for GCSE

Book F1 part A

PATHFINDER EDITION

PUBLISHED BY THE PRESS SYNDICATE OF THE UNIVERSITY OF CAMBRIDGE
The Pitt Building, Trumpington Street, Cambridge, United Kingdom

CAMBRIDGE UNIVERSITY PRESS
The Edinburgh Building, Cambridge CB2 2RU, UK
40 West 20th Street, New York, NY 10011-4211, USA
10 Stamford Road, Oakleigh, VIC 3166, Australia
Ruiz de Alarcón 13, 28014 Madrid, Spain
Dock House, The Waterfront, Cape Town 8001, South Africa

http://www.cambridge.org

© The School Mathematics Project 2001
First published 2001
Reprinted 2001

Printed in Italy by Rotolito Lombarda
Typeface Minion   *System* QuarkXPress®

A catalogue record for this book is available from the British Library

ISBN 0 521 01198 1   paperback

Typesetting and technical illustrations by The School Mathematics Project

Acknowledgements

The authors and publishers are grateful to the following Examination Boards
for permission to reproduce questions from past examination papers:
Edexcel   Edexcel Foundation
OCR(MEG)   Oxford, Cambridge and RSA Examinations

We have been unable to trace the copyright holder of the photograph on page
114 (from *Eagle Book of Cars and Motor Sport* [London: Hulton Press, 1958],
p. 43), and would be grateful for any information that would enable us to
do so.

Contents

1 Rooms

This work will help you to

♦ find areas of rectangles with whole number or decimal lengths
♦ find areas of shapes made from rectangles
♦ change between centimetres and metres

A Tiles

A1 These rectangles have been drawn on centimetre squared paper.
Find the area of each one in cm².

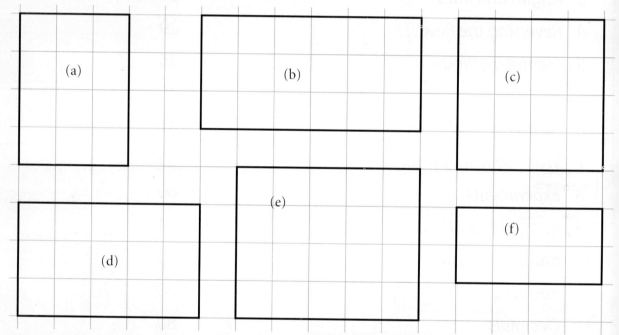

A2 These tiles are used to make mosaics.
Measure each tile and find its area.

 A   B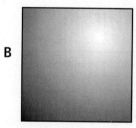

A3 Sanjay wants to put mosaic tiles on a table top.
The table top measures 60 cm by 90 cm.

(a) What is the area of the table top?

(b) How many tiles of size A would he need to cover the table top?

(c) How many tiles of size B would he need to cover the table top?

A4 These are different tiles for walls.
Find the area of each tile.

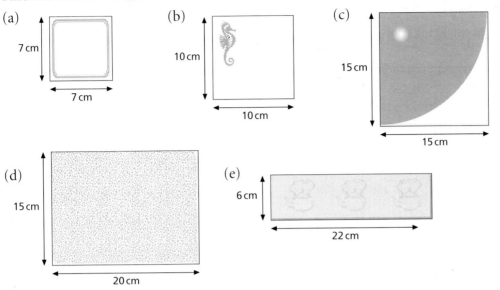

(a) 7 cm, 7 cm

(b) 10 cm, 10 cm

(c) 15 cm, 15 cm

(d) 15 cm, 20 cm

(e) 6 cm, 22 cm

Floor tiles

Here are a range of stone tiles which can be used on floors.
Find the area of each of these tiles.

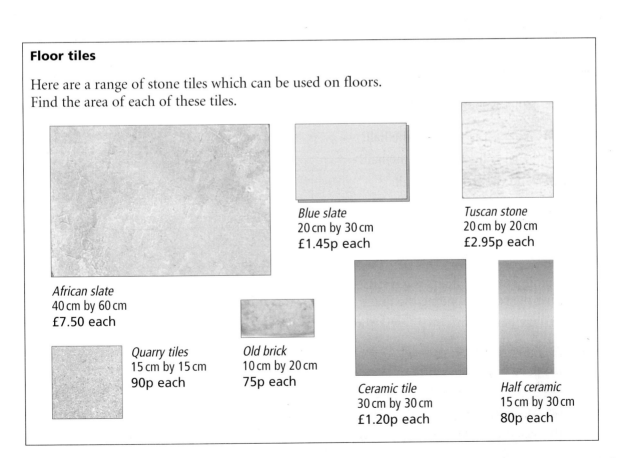

African slate
40 cm by 60 cm
£7.50 each

Blue slate
20 cm by 30 cm
£1.45p each

Tuscan stone
20 cm by 20 cm
£2.95p each

Quarry tiles
15 cm by 15 cm
90p each

Old brick
10 cm by 20 cm
75p each

Ceramic tile
30 cm by 30 cm
£1.20p each

Half ceramic
15 cm by 30 cm
80p each

ⓑ *Floor space*

This is the plan of a flat.

The area of the living room is
$4.5 \times 3 = 13.5 \ \text{m}^2$.

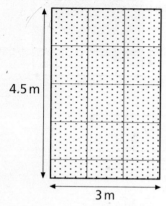

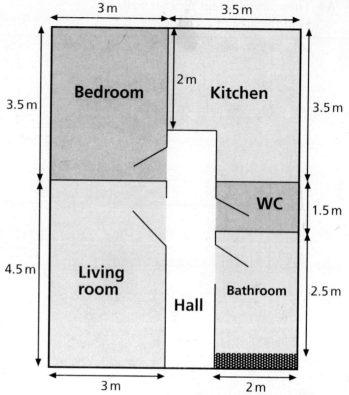

B1 Find the area of floor in

   (a) the bedroom

   (b) the bathroom

   (c) the WC

B2 (a) Draw a sketch of the kitchen.
On your sketch draw a line to split the kitchen into 2 rectangles.

   (b) Find the area of these two rectangles.

   (c) What is the area of the floor in the kitchen?

B3 (a) What is the width of the hall?

   (b) What is the length of the hall?

   (c) Find the area of the hall.

B4 The cost of cleaning a carpet is £5 per square metre.
How much would it cost to clean the carpets in

   (a) the bedroom   (b) the living room   (c) the hall?

B5 Sanding wooden floors is advertised at £7.50 per square metre.
Find the cost of sanding the floors in

   (a) the bathroom   (b) the WC   (c) the kitchen

B6 One litre of sealant covers $1.5 \ \text{m}^2$ of wooden floor.
It can be bought in 1 litre or 2.5 litre size cans.
A 1 litre can costs £5.99.   A 2.5 litre can costs £12.99.

   (a) What area will a 2.5 litre tin of paint cover?

   (b) What is the cheapest way to buy enough sealant to cover the bathroom floor?

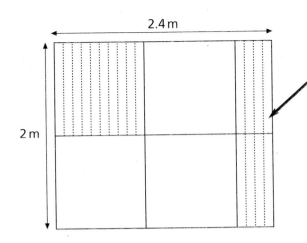

This rectangle measures 2 m by 2.4 m.

Each of these strip is $\frac{1}{10}$ or $0.1\,m^2$.

There are 4 whole square metres and 8 strips of $0.1\,m^2$.

The area of the rectangle is therefore $4.8\,m^2$.

B7 Use your calculator to check the area of the rectangle above.

B8 Here is the plan of another flat.

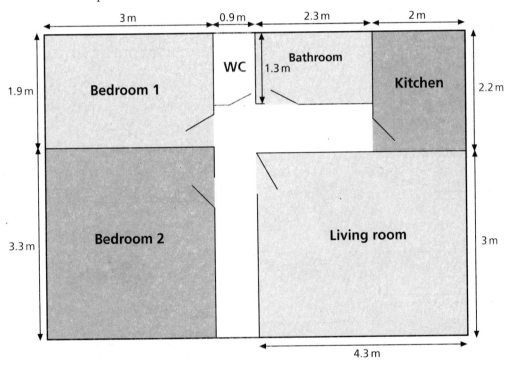

Use a calculator to find the area of the floors in these rooms of this flat.

(a) bedroom 1   (b) bedroom 2

(c) the living room   (d) the kitchen

B9 (a) The WC is 0.9 m by 1.3 m
Estimate the area of the WC.

(b) Use your calculator to find the area of a the WC exactly.

B10 Use your calculator to find the area of the bathroom.

C *Composite shapes*

The area of this floor can be found by splitting
the shape into rectangles.

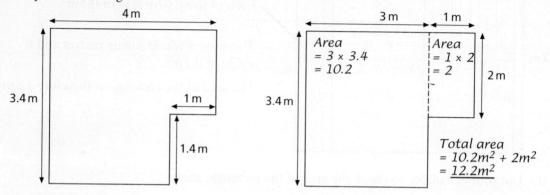

C1 Draw a sketch of these floors with lines splitting them into rectangles.
Work out the area of each floor, showing all your working.

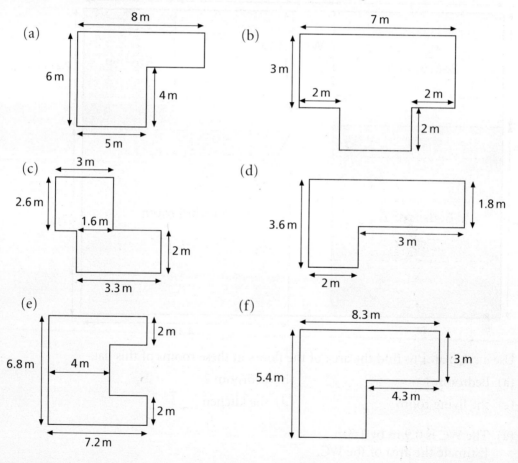

C2 A carpenter is going to put skirting board around the edge of the rooms in C1.
Find the total length of skirting board for each of these floors.

A decorator wants to know how much paint she needs to paint a room with a window.

This plan shows the measurements of the wall.

The area of this rectangle

is $3\,\text{m} \times 2.3\,\text{m} = 6.9\ \text{m}^2$

However, the area of the window is:

$2\,\text{m} \times 1.6\,\text{m} = 3.2\ \text{m}^2$

So the area of the room that needs to be painted is

$6.9\ \text{m}^2 - 3.2\ \text{m}^2 = 3.7\ \text{m}^2.$

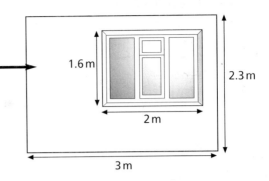

C3 Find the area that would need painting on these walls:

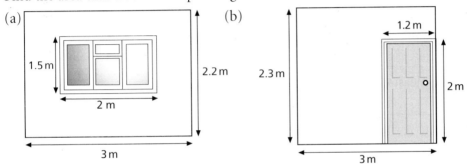

(a)

(b)

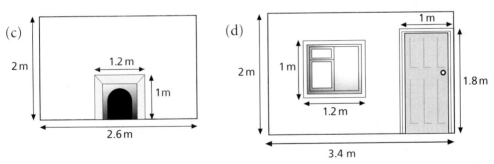

(c)

(d)

C4 A tin of paint covers an area of $8\,\text{m}^2$ with one coat.

Which of the walls in C3 could be covered by a tin of paint if two coats were given?

C5 This garden pond has a path all round it.

  (a) Find the area of the pond.

  (b) Find the area of the path.

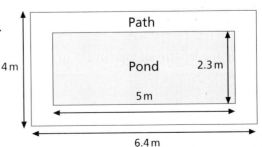

D Mixed measurements

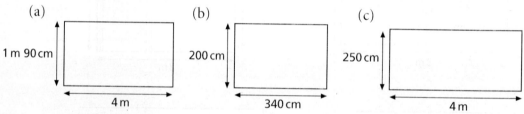

D1 These measurements are in centimetres.
Write them as decimals of a metre.

(a) 70 cm   (b) 90 cm   (c) 95 cm   (d) 1 m 10 cm

(e) 75 cm   (f) 63 cm   (g) 29 cm   (h) 1 m 25 cm

(i) 2 m 84 cm   (j) 5 cm   (k) 1 m 5 cm   (l) 2 m 8 cm

D2 Write these measurements in metres and centimetres without decimals

(a) 0.8 m   (b) 0.6 m   (c) 0.25 m   (d) 1.5 m

(e) 3.75 m   (f) 2.84 m   (g) 0.04 m   (h) 5.08 m

D3 By changing measurements into decimals of metres, find the areas of these walls in m².

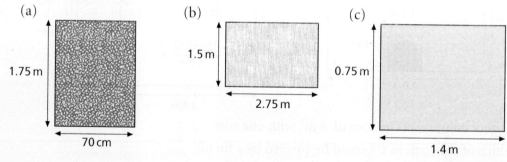

(a) 1 m 90 cm / 4 m   (b) 200 cm / 340 cm   (c) 250 cm / 4 m

D4 Work out the areas of these carpet remnants in cm².

(a) 1.75 m / 70 cm   (b) 1.5 m / 2.75 m   (c) 0.75 m / 1.4 m

D5 The carpets in D4 are to have tape around the edges.
What length of tape is needed for each carpet in centimetres?

D6 Write the lengths of tape in D5 in metres.

Test yourself with these questions

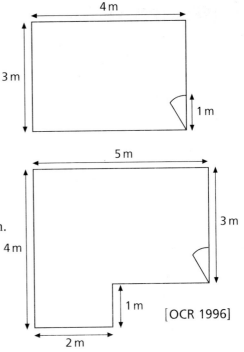

T1 This is floor plan of Justin's bedroom. The position of the door is marked.

(a) Work out the area of the floor.

(b) The room has a skirting-board at the bottom of the walls. It goes all round the room but not across the door.

How long is the skirting-board?

(c) This is a floor plan of Tammy's bedroom. Work out the area of the floor.

[OCR 1996]

T2 Find the shaded area.

(a)

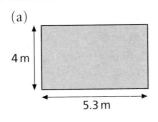

(b)

(c)

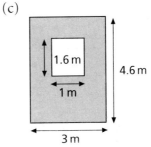

T3 This diagram shows the floor plan of a room.

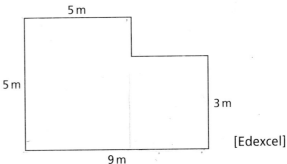

Work out the area of the floor.
Give the units with your answer.

[Edexcel]

T4 A rectangular carpet measures 120 cm by 1.5 m.

(a) Find the area of the carpet in cm^2.

(b) Find the area of the carpet in m^2.

2 Weather watching

This work will help you to

◆ read line graphs and bar charts

◆ construct frequency tables

◆ find the mode, median, mean and range of a set of data

A Winter and summer

This data shows the weather on a day in August and a day in January around the world.

World Weather

August 16th 1999

	Weather	Temp °C		Weather	Temp °C		Weather	Temp °C
Algiers	s	32	Copenhagen	sh	15	New York	c	27
Amsterdam	f	18	Dublin	f	16	Port Stanley	c	3
Athens	s	33	Funchal	f	26	Reykjavik	c	13
Bahrain	s	46	Hong Kong	c	32	Rio de Jan.	c	13
Beijing	s	32	Johannesburg	s	21	Santiago	s	19
Berlin	sh	19	Madrid	s	34	Singapore	c	28
Bermuda	f	30	Melbourne	c	11	Sydney	s	13
Buenos Aires	c	8	Miami	c	27	Tokyo	f	31
Budapest	c	25	Moscow	sh	18	Toronto	c	17
Cairo	s	35	Nairobi	c	18	Vancouver	c	18
Chicago	c	21	New Delhi	s	34	Wellington	c	14

Jan 23rd 2000

	Weather	Temp °C		Weather	Temp °C		Weather	Temp °C
Algiers	r	12	Copenhagen	c	−1	New York	s	−8
Amsterdam	f	3	Dublin	f	6	Port Stanley	f	18
Athens	r	9	Funchal	c	17	Reykjavik	c	2
Bahrain	f	21	Hong Kong	r	19	Rio de Jan.	f	30
Beijing	s	−4	Johannesburg	c	23	Santiago	s	28
Berlin	s	−6	Madrid	s	8	Singapore	c	28
Bermuda	c	14	Melbourne	f	15	Sydney	f	20
Buenos Aires	f	27	Miami	c	21	Tokyo	s	8
Budapest	c	−4	Moscow	f	−15	Toronto	s	−17
Cairo	s	18	Nairobi	c	25	Vancouver	m	4
Chicago	sn	−7	New Delhi	s	19	Wellington	c	22

s - sunny   **c** - cloudy   **f** - fair   **r** - rain   **sh** - showers   **sn** - snow   **m** - mist

A1 What was the temperature, in °C, on August 16th 1999 in

    (a) Melbourne   (b) Cairo   (c) Port Stanley

A2 What was the temperature, in °C, on January 23rd 2000 in

    (a) Rio de Janiero   (b) New York   (c) Moscow

A3 On January 23rd 2000 the weather in Copenhagen was cloudy and just below freezing.
Describe the weather in:

    (a) Hong Kong on August 16th 1999   (b) Toronto on January 23rd 2000

A4 (a) Which place had the same temperature on both days?

    (b) Give the names of three places which were warmer in January than in August.

    (c) Why are some places warmer in January than in August?

A5 List these places in order of temperature on the 23rd January, warmest first.

    Amsterdam, Berlin, Chicago, Dublin, New York, Moscow, Wellington

A6 Algiers was 20 degrees colder in January than in August.
Write a similar sentence for

    (a) Santiago   (b) Reykjavik   (c) Funchal

    (d) Copenhagen   (e) Berlin   (f) Moscow

A7 (a) What was the temperature in Amsterdam on 23rd January 2000?

    (b) On the 22nd, the day before, it was 2 degrees warmer.
        What was the temperature on the day before?

    Find the temperature on the 22nd January,

    (c) if it was 3 degrees colder in Bahrain than it was on the 23rd

    (d) if it was 1 degree warmer in Budapest than it was on the 23rd

    (e) if it was 4 degrees warmer in Berlin than it was on the 23rd

    (f) if it was 3 degrees colder in Beijing than it was on the 23rd

A8 There was 6 degrees difference in temperature between
August and January in Miami.
What were the differences in temperature between August and January in

    (a) Bermuda   (b) Bahrain   (c) Beijing

    (d) Toronto   (e) New York   (f) Chicago

A9 Which place had the biggest difference in temperature between August and January?

Ⓑ *Rain or shine*

This graph shows the average highest temperature for Moscow and Melbourne each month.

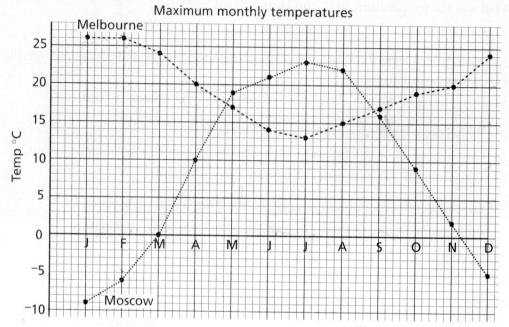

B1 What is the average highest temperature in Melbourne in

(a) January   (b) June   (c) September

B2 What is the average highest temperature in Moscow in

(a) January   (b) June   (c) September

B3 During which months is the average temperature warmer in Moscow than in Melbourne?

B4 What is the difference in average temperature between Melbourne and Moscow in

(a) June   (b) December   (c) February

B5 In which month is the difference between the average temperatures in the two cities

(a) the most   (b) the least

B6 Here are the average highest temperatures in °C each month for Ottawa (Canada) and Buenos Aires (Argentina).

	Jan	Feb	Mar	Apr	May	Jun	Jul	Aug	Sept	Oct	Nov	Dec
Ottawa	⁻6	⁻6	1	11	19	24	27	25	20	12	4	⁻4
Buenos Aires	29	28	26	22	18	14	14	16	18	21	24	28

Draw a line graph like the one above to show the temperatures in these two cities.

This bar graph shows the average monthly rainfall in cm for London.

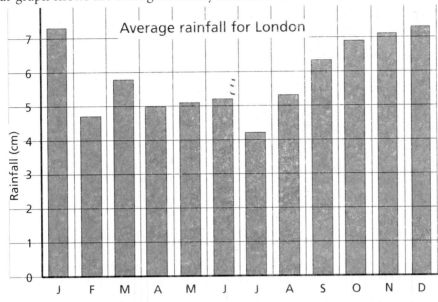

B7 What does one small unit on the rainfall scale stand for?

B8 What is the average monthly rainfall in London in:

(a) April (b) June (c) September?

B9 (a) Which two months have the highest average rainfall in London?

(b) What is the average monthly rainfall for each of these months?

These are the average monthly rainfall figures for Manchester.

Month	Jan	Feb	Mar	Apr	May	Jun	Jul	Aug	Sept	Oct	Nov	Dec
Rainfall (cm)	6.4	4.6	5.6	4.7	5.5	6.2	6.0	7.3	6.8	7.1	7.2	7.2

B10 In what month does it rain most on average in Manchester?

B11 In Manchester in February the average rainfall is 4.6 cm.
How much more rain is there on average in

(a) April (b) June (c) August

B12 In which months does it rain more on average in London than in Manchester?

B13 What is the total average rainfall in Manchester for June, July and August.

B14 Some people in London say that it always rains more in Manchester. Is this true?
Why might people think that this was true?

Information about rainfall and temperature is often given on the same graph.
Here is a graph of rainfall and temperature for Hong Kong.
On this graph the rainfall scale is on the left and the temperature scale is on the right.

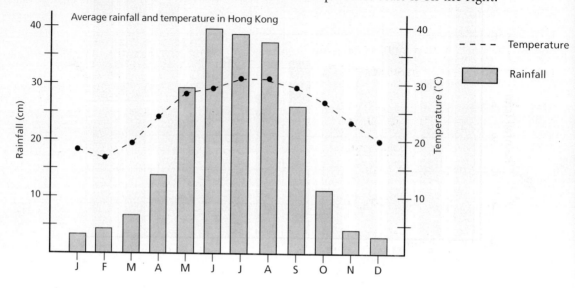

B15 (a) Roughly how many centimetres of rain fall on average in Hong Kong in August?
Is this more or less than Manchester in August?

(b) Which month of the year has the highest rainfall?

(c) Which two months of the year have the highest average temperature?

B16 Are these statements true or false for the weather in Hong Kong?

A: *Don't go there in December as this is the coldest and wettest time of the year.*

B: *The warmest months are also the wettest months.*

C: *At least it doesn't rain as much as it does in Manchester.*

B17 Which of the above statements are true for this graph of Vancouver?

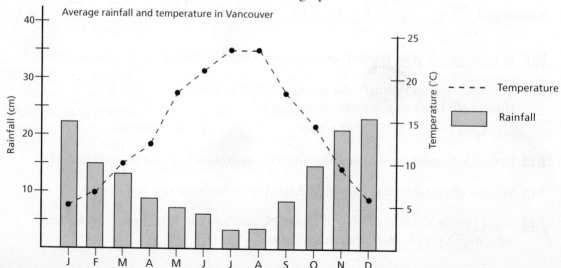

C Frequency

Wind is always described by the direction it is coming from.

This diagram shows the number of days in August 1999 that it blew from each direction.

The data was recorded in Sussex, England.

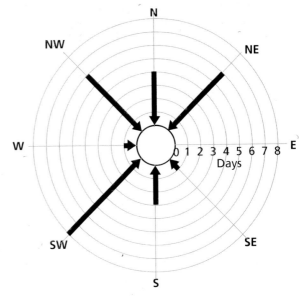

C1 What was the least frequent direction the wind blew from in August?

C2 What was the frequency with which it blew from the South East?

C3 What was the modal wind direction for August?

> The **mode** or **modal** value is the value with the highest frequency.

C4 Here is the wind direction data at Sussex University for February 1999.

Days	1	2	3	4	5	6	7	8	9	10	11	12	13	14	15
Wind	NW	NW	W	NW	W	NW	NW	NE	NE	NW	N	S	N	N	W

	16	17	18	19	20	21	22	23	24	25	26	27	28
	NW	W	NW	SW	W	W	NW	NW	NE	W	SW	W	W

(a) Copy and complete this frequency table for the wind direction in February.

Direction	Tally	Frequency
N	///	
NE		

(b) What was the modal wind direction for February 1999?

(c) Draw a wind direction diagram for February like the one for August.

C5 The weather at 30 weather stations around the UK on 9th March 2000 was listed as

sunny	sunny	rain	cloudy	cloudy	sunny
drizzle	drizzle	cloudy	cloudy	cloudy	dull
sunny	cloudy	showers	sunny	cloudy	sunny
drizzle	cloudy	dull	rain	dull	sunny
cloudy	sunny	sunny	cloudy	sunny	sunny

(a) Make a frequency table for the different types of weather on this day.

(b) What is the frequency of the weather being recorded as drizzle?

(c) Use your table to draw a bar graph of weather types.

(d) What was the modal type of weather on this day?

C6 The amount of cloud at any time is measured on a scale 0 to 8.
This says how many eighths or 'oktas' of the sky are covered in cloud.
This data lists the cloud cover at midday for the days of August 1999
on Fair Isle (Scotland).

1, 0, 1, 1, 7, 5, 7, 7, 7, 4, 6, 6, 8, 6, 2, 5, 7, 7, 5, 7, 3, 7, 7, 1, 7, 8, 6, 8, 6, 8, 8,

(a) Complete this frequency table for the oktas of cloud cover in August 1999.

(b) What is the modal number of oktas cloud cover?

Number of oktas	Tally	Frequency
0		
1		
2		

(c) Copy and complete this bar chart on centimetre squared paper.

(d) Are these statements true or false for Fair Isle in August 1999?

   (i) *The sky was more than half covered in cloud for most days of the month.*

   (ii) *There were no days without cloud in August.*

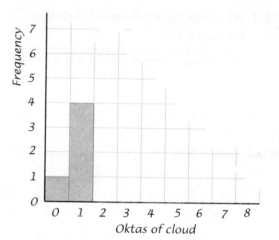

C7 The number of days on which it rained in the last half of August 1999
for the 30 weather stations in question C5 was also recorded:

5 10 8 5 5 3 5 6 5 5 4 4 7 8 8
3 5 7 7 5 6 8 4 7 4 5 6 7 9 4

(a) Make a frequency table for the number of rainy days in this period.

(b) Use your table to draw a bar chart for the number of rainy days.

(c) What was the mode of the number of rainy days in this period?

Mean and range

The mean of a set of data is the total of all the data divided by
the number of pieces of data there are.

The mean of 5, 12, 3, 4, 3, 6 is $(5 + 12 + 3 + 4 + 3 + 6) \div 6 = 6.5$

The range of a set of data is the difference between the largest and smallest
value in the data.

The range of 5, 12, 3, 4, 3, 6 is $12 - 3 = 9$

D Comparing East and West

This data shows the weather at some places on the East and West sides
of England and Wales on August 16th 1999.

East	Sun(hrs)	Rain(mm)	Temp(°C)
Scarborough	11.1	0.3	19
Newcastle	9.2	0.3	18
Cleethorpes	8.0	0.3	19
Skegness	7.4	5.1	20
Hunstanton	4.6	0.8	19
Cromer	5.9	2.0	20
Norwich	7.3	15.5	20
Lowestoft	7.3	6.1	19
Clacton	10.3	8.9	19
Margate	8.5	0.5	21

West	Sun(hrs)	Rain(mm)	Temp(°C)
Newquay	3.3	0.8	17
Bristol	7.1	0	19
Ross on Wye	9.5	0	19
Southport	5.0	17.8	18
Morecambe	5.4	3.3	16
Isle of Man	9.0	0.3	18
Keswick	1.3	7.9	14
Anglesey	11.0	0.5	18
Colwyn Bay	9.8	0	17
Tenby	7.4	0	19

D1 (a) What was the mean temperature of the places in the East on this day?

(b) What was the mean temperature of the places in the West on this day?

(c) Did the East or West have the higher mean temperature?

(d) Find the range of temperatures for (i) the East (ii) the West.

(e) Was the greatest range of temperatures in the East or West?

D2 (a) Find the mean number of hours of sunshine for (i) the East (ii) the West.

(b) Which group of places had the highest mean number of hours of sunshine?

(c) Which group had the highest range of hours of sunshine?

D3 (a) Which group of places on August 16th 1999 had the highest mean rainfall?

(b) Which group had the highest range of rainfall?

D4 The table below shows the weather for the same places on January 23rd 2000.

(a) Find the means and ranges for sunshine, rainfall and temperature in the East.

(b) Find the means and ranges for sunshine, rainfall and temperature in the West.

(c) Compare the weather in the East and West on January 23rd 2000.

East	Sun(hrs)	Rain(mm)	Temp(°C)
Scarborough	1.5	3.0	5
Newcastle	1.9	1.0	5
Cleethorpes	2.9	1.3	5
Skegness	3.3	1.8	5
Hunstanton	2.3	2.8	5
Cromer	2.5	1.3	6
Norwich	2.4	1.5	6
Lowestoft	1.0	1.3	6
Clacton	4.4	0.5	7
Margate	2.0	1.6	5

West	Sun(hrs)	Rain(mm)	Temp(°C)
Newquay	3.3	0	9
Bristol	2.1	0.4	9
Ross on Wye	4.5	0.2	8
Southport	5.5	0.1	8
Morecambe	4.6	0.3	7
Isle of Man	6.0	0.7	8
Keswick	1.5	0.2	6
Anglesey	4.1	0.4	8
Colwyn Bay	3.9	1.0	8
Tenby	2.4	0.1	9

Test yourself with these questions

This data shows the weather for Fair Isle during the last two weeks of December 1999

	Week One								Week Two						
	18	19	20	21	22	23	24		25	26	27	28	29	30	31
Highest temp (°C)	1	3	5	7	8	8	7		6	5	6	6	6	7	8
Lowest temp (°C)	⁻4	⁻4	⁻2	⁻1	4	2	5		2	2	0	2	2	0	⁻1
Cloud (oktas)	7	3	5	8	8	7	4		8	8	7	5	2	7	7

T1 What is the difference between the highest and lowest temperatures on the

  (a) 23rd Dec   (b) 21st Dec   (c) 19th Dec

T2 On what day was the difference between the highest and lowest temperature the most?

T3 On the same scales draw a line graph of (i) the highest temperature
                                              (ii) the lowest temperature

T4 (a) Copy and complete this frequency table for the amount of cloud over the two weeks.

Number of oktas	Tally	Frequency
0		
1		
2		

  (b) Use your frequency table to draw a bar graph showing cloud cover.
  (c) What is the modal amount of cloud cover for this fortnight?

T5 (a) Find the mean of the highest temperature in week one.
  (b) What is the range of the highest temperatures in week one?
  (c) Find the mean and range of the highest temperature for week two.
  (d) Which week had the highest mean temperature?

3 Angles and lines

This will help you to practise measuring angles and describing types of angles.
You will learn about

◆ angles on a straight line and around a point
◆ the angles inside a triangle
◆ how to draw a triangle given some lengths and angles

A Angles and lines

Are you being obtuse?

Make an angle using two lines which is

• acute   • obtuse   • reflex

Ask someone to check them for you.

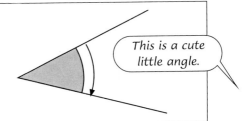

This is a cute little angle.

Estimating angles

Estimate the angles below using two lines.

30°   60°   45°   90°

120°   180°   210°   270°   300°

Check your angles with an angle measurer.
Keep a table of each angle and your estimate.

Angles on a straight line

Place one line so that the end of it lies about
half way along another as this diagram shows.

Measure the two angles that are made.

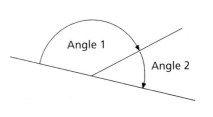

Angle 1

Angle 2

Move the lines to other positions where
one line still lies touching the other.

What do you notice about the two angles each time?

A1 For each of the angles in this diagram
- say whether it is acute, obtuse or reflex
- estimate the angle roughly
- check your estimate with an angle measurer

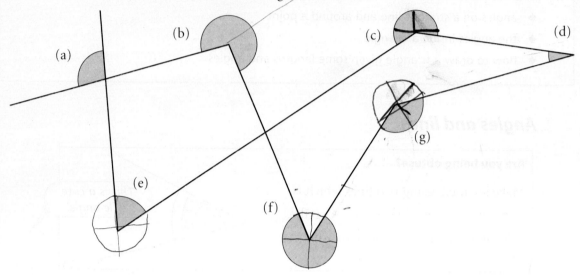

A2 (a) Measure each of the angles on these pieces.

(b) Which pairs of pieces could make a straight line?

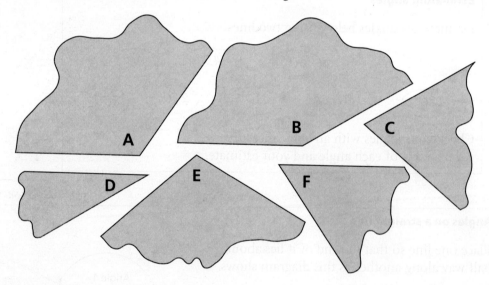

A3 (a) Could you make a straight line with two acute angles?

(b) Which of these pairs could make a straight line?

acute + obtuse   obtuse + obtuse   right-angle + right-angle

> Angles which meet to make a straight line
> must add up to 180°.
>
> a / b
>
> *Angle a + angle b = 180°*

A4 Work out the missing angles in these diagrams.
  Do not measure as the diagrams are not accurate.

 a / 65°

 b 130°

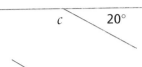 c 20°

d 47°

60° e

150° f

19° g 96°

25° h 83°

100° i 30°

A5 Use the instructions below to make
a full size copy of this pattern.

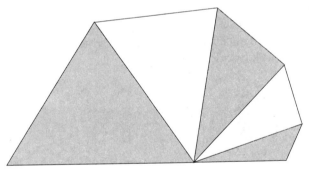

> 1 Draw a line 10 cm long.
>
> ———————
>
> 10 cm

> 2 Measure an angle of 54°.
>
>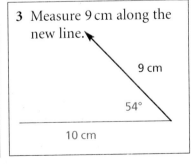
>
> 54°
>
> 10 cm

> 3 Measure 9 cm along the
>   new line.
>
> 9 cm
>
> 54°
>
> 10 cm

> 4 Measure an angle of 45°.
>   Draw a line 8 cm long.
>
> 9 cm
> 8 cm
> 45°
> 54°
>
> 10 cm

Continue with: Angle 36° then line 7 cm
          Angle 27° then line 6 cm
          Angle 18° then line 5 cm

Join the ends of the lines to complete the pattern.

B Angles round a point

Fitting round a point

This equilateral triangle, square and regular hexagon have sides with the same length.

Measure the internal angles shown on each shape.

The picture below shows the triangle, two squares and the hexagon around a dot.
What is the sum of all the angles around the dot?

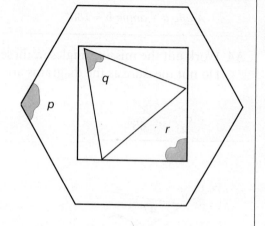

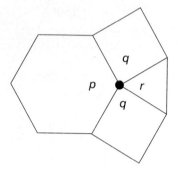

What other ways can you fit these shapes round a point without gaps or overlapping? Sheet P15 has several copies of these shapes. Cut these out and investigate.

What is the sum of the angles round the point each time?

B1 The cheeses below have had pieces cut out from them.
Which slice has been cut from which circle?
Check by adding the angles.

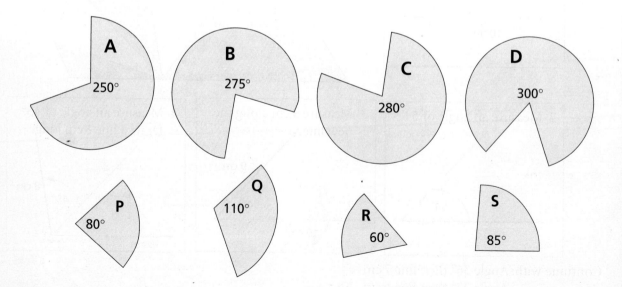

B2 Calculate the angles marked with letters in these diagrams

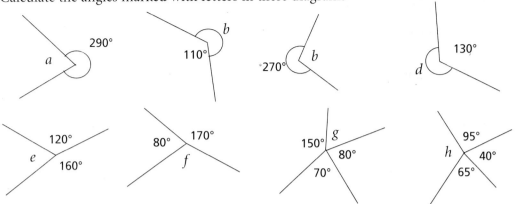

B3 In this circle a line was drawn from the centre to the top of the circle.
Two more lines were then drawn from the centre at angles of 120° from the previous line.

(a) Calculate angle *a*.

(b) If you joined up the three points on the edge of the circle, what special triangle would you get?

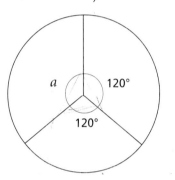

B4 What angle would you have to use inside a circle in B3 so that the points on the edge made a square?

B5 (a) What angle would you use inside a circle to give 5 points on the edge which join to make a regular pentagon?

(b) Draw a circle of radius 8 cm.
Use an angle measurer to draw a regular pentagon in the circle.

B6 Use the method of drawing lines inside a circle to draw:

(a) a regular hexagon (6 sides)   (b) a regular octagon (8 sides)

B7 What angle would you use inside a circle to draw:

(a) a regular dodecagon (12 sides)   (b) a regular icosagon (20 sides)

Star patterns

The first of these patterns is drawn using a circle with 5 points equally spaced around the edge.

The second uses a circle with 9 equally spaced points.

Draw some patterns of your own using circles with different number of equally spaced points.

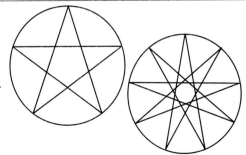

ℂ *Triangles*

What happens when you put the
angles of a triangle together?

Does this work for all triangles?

What does this tell you about the
angles in a triangle?

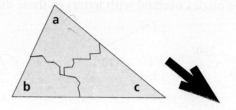

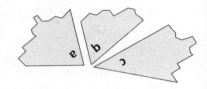

C1 Calculate the missing angles in these triangles.

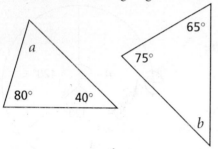

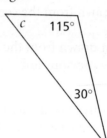

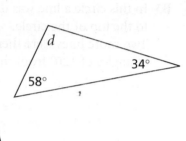

C2 These triangles are all right-angled triangles.
Calculate the missing angles.

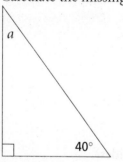

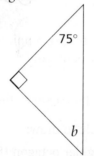

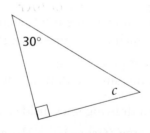

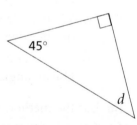

C3 These are all isosceles triangles.
Calculate the missing angles.

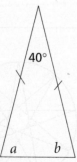

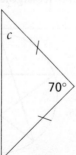

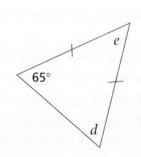

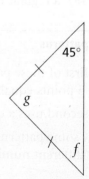

C4 What size are the internal angles of an equilateral triangle? Explain how you worked this out.

C5 (a) If in this diagram angle $a = 55°$ and $b = 80°$, what would angle c be?

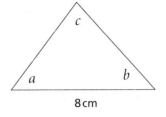

(b) Make a full size copy of this drawing with $a = 55°$ and $b = 80°$.
Measure angle c to check the accuracy of your drawing.

(c) If in this diagram angle $a = 35°$ and $b = 110°$, what would angle c be?
Draw an accurate diagram and check angle c.

C6 This pattern has been drawn by drawing 6 triangles like those in C5 using the same base. The angles in the triangles are:

- $a = 15°$ and $b = 10°$
- $a = 30°$ and $b = 20°$
- $a = 45°$ and $b = 30°$
- $a = 60°$ and $b = 40°$
- $a = 75°$ and $b = 50°$
- $a = 90°$ and $b = 60°$

Copy this pattern using a base of 10 cm.

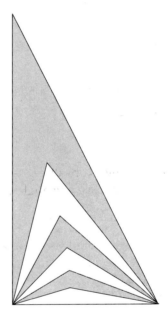

*C7 Find all the angles marked with letters in this diagram.

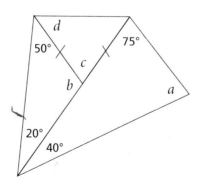

Test yourself with these questions

T1 Work out the missing angles in these diagrams.

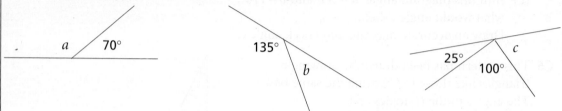

T2 Calculate the missing angles in these diagrams.

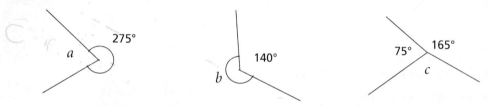

T3 What angle would you have to use at the centre of a circle to draw a regular 15 sided shape inside the circle?

T4 Find the missing angles in these triangles.

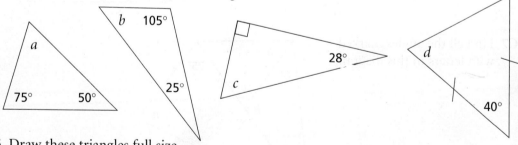

T5 Draw these triangles full size.

(a)   (b)

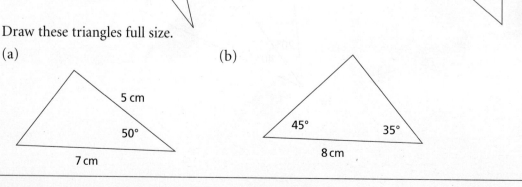

4 Reversing the flow

You should know that

- $\frac{a}{5}$ means $a \div 5$, $5a$ means $5 \times a$
- $2n - 5$ means 'multiply n by 2 and then take off 5'

This work will help you learn how to

- solve an arrow diagram puzzle by reversing the diagram.
- turn an arrow diagram into an equation.
- solve an equation using arrow diagrams.
- write and solve an equation for a number puzzle.

A Mathematical whispers

TG

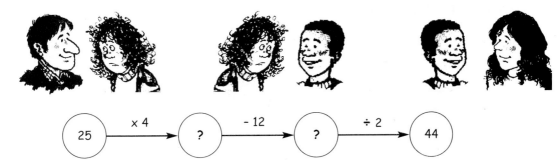

A1 Copy and complete each of these mathematical whispers.
Do them without using a calculator.

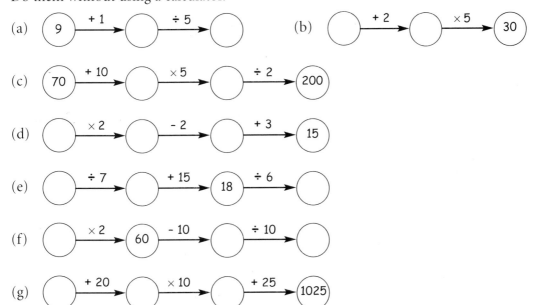

A2 Dave starts a mathematical whisper.

| He thinks of a number and adds 6.  | Jo takes Dave's answer and multiplies by 3.  | Raj adds 10 to Jo's answer. Raj ends up with 40. |

(a) Copy and complete this arrow diagram for the whisper.

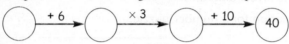

(b) What number did Dave think of?

A3 Draw arrow diagrams for each of these whispers.
For each one, work out what number Dave started with.

(a)

| Dave thinks of a number and subtracts 9.  | Jo takes Dave's answer and divides by 5.  | Raj adds 10 to Jo's answer. Raj ends up with 13. |

(b)

| Dave thinks of a number and divides by 2. | Jo takes Dave's answer and multiplies by 3. | Raj divides Jo's answer by 12 and ends up with 5. |

A4 Copy and complete these whispers, using a calculator if you need.

(a)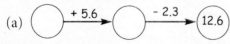

(b)

(c)

(d)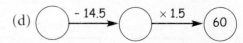

Ⓑ *Using letters*

To solve this puzzle...

... we can use a letter to stand for the number that goes into the puzzle.

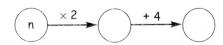

In each box we can show what happens to the letter.

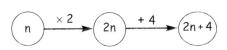

So the puzzle can be written...

2n + 4 = 10

We call this **an equation**.

B1 Suppose the letter *n* goes into each of these puzzles.
Match each puzzle with its equation.

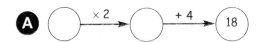

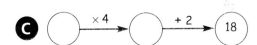

P $\boxed{4n + 2 = 18}$

Q $\boxed{\dfrac{n}{2} + 4 = 18}$

R $\boxed{2n + 4 = 18}$

B2 Which of the equations below matches this puzzle?

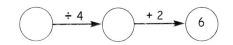

K $\boxed{\dfrac{n}{2} + 4 = 6}$ **L** $\boxed{\dfrac{n}{4} + 2 = 6}$ **M** $\boxed{4n + 2 = 6}$ **N** $\boxed{2n + 4 = 6}$

B3 Which of the puzzles below matches the equation $3x - 2 = 16$?

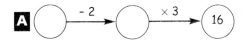

B4 Draw a puzzle for each of these equations.

(a) $3n - 4 = 8$

(b) $\dfrac{a}{5} + 7 = 9$

B5 Write down an equation for each of these puzzles.
Choose your own letters to stand for the numbers that go into the puzzles.

(a)

(b)

(c)

(d)

C *Solving equations*

Solving the equation $3y + 9 = 45$ means finding what number y stands for.
We are finding what number fits the equation.

You can do this by first writing the equation as an arrow diagram.
Then just reverse the flow of the arrow diagram.

- Draw an arrow diagram for the equation.

- Reverse the arrow diagram to find the value of y.

- Check that your value of y works in the original equation.

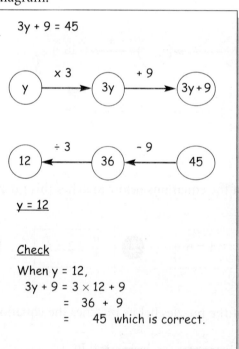

C1 (a) Copy and complete this working to solve the equation $9k - 3 = 15$.

(b) Check that your answer works in the original equation.

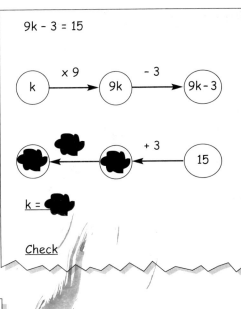

$9k - 3 = 15$

Check

C2 $\frac{a}{4} + 12 = 20$

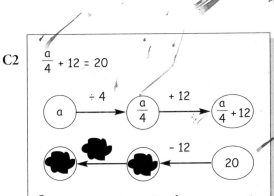

Copy and complete this working to solve the equation $\frac{a}{4} + 12 = 20$.

C3 Draw an arrow diagram for each of these equations.
Then reverse the diagram and solve the equation.

Try not to use a calculator, and check each of your solutions.

(a) $7n - 5 = 23$ (b) $5x + 3 = 68$

(c) $8p - 5 = 43$ (d) $4y + 12 = 60$

C4 Use reverse arrow diagrams to solve each of these equations.

(a) $\frac{w}{4} - 16 = 4$ (b) $\frac{m}{2} + 6 = 10$ (c) $\frac{x}{5} - 2 = 3$

C5 Solve each of these equations.
You may need to use a calculator.

(a) $3a - 5 = 3.4$ (b) $2n + 1.5 = 13.9$

(c) $2.5y - 3 = 62$ (d) $\frac{k}{4} - 1.8 = 2.7$

D Number puzzles

Suppose *n* stands for the number that Mary first thinks of.

Then we can write the number puzzle as an equation. $2n + 3 = 31$

We can also show the puzzle as an arrow diagram.

Now we can reverse the arrow diagram
to solve the equation and find Mary's number.

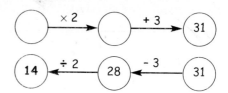

D1 Here is a number puzzle.

> I think of a number.
> - I multiply by 4.
> - I take off 6.
> My answer is 22.
> What was my number?

(a) Copy and complete this equation $\bullet n - \bullet = 22$
for the number puzzle.

(b) Write down an arrow diagram for the equation.

(c) Write down a reverse arrow diagram.

(d) Use the reverse arrow diagram to solve the number puzzle.

D2 Write an equation for each of these number puzzles.
Then solve your equation using arrow diagrams.

(a)
> I think of a number.
> - I multiply by 5.
> - I subtract 8.
> My answer is 97.
> What was my number?

(b)
> I think of a number.
> - I divide by 7.
> - I add 2.
> My answer is 10.
> What was my number?

(c)
> I think of a number.
> - I divide by 4.
> - I subtract 5.
> My answer is 47.
> What was my number?

D3 Write down a number puzzle of your own.
Make sure you can find the answer!

Now give someone else your puzzle to solve.

D4 (a) Write down a number puzzle for the equation $3n - 4 = 20$.

(b) Solve the equation using an arrow diagram.

D5 Use arrow diagrams to solve these equations.

(a) $4x + 3.5 = 9.9$ (b) $3n + 2.2 = 12.7$ (c) $1.5k + 4 = 10$

Test yourself with these questions

T1 Without using a calculator, copy and complete these arrow diagrams.

(a)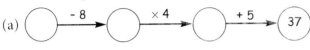

(b)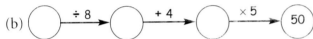

T2 Draw an arrow diagram for each of these equations.
Then reverse the arrow diagram and solve the equation.

(a) $3m - 6 = 18$ (b) $4s + 2 = 30$

(c) $\dfrac{w}{2} - 4 = 10$ (d) $\dfrac{v}{5} - 4 = 6$

T3 Write an equation for each of these number puzzles.
Then solve your equation using arrow diagrams.

(a)
> *I think of a number.*
> - *I multiply by 4.*
> - *I subtract 2.*
>
> *My answer is 30.*
> *What was my number?*

(b)
> *I think of a number.*
> - *I divide by 2.*
> - *I subtract 10.*
>
> *My answer is 17.*
> *What was my number?*

5 Mental methods

This will give you practice in mutiplying by 10, 100, 1000 and by numbers like 30, 200, ...

You should also learn

◆ how to round a whole number to one significant figure

◆ how to estimate the answer to a multiplication by rounding the numbers

A Multiplying and dividing by 10, 100, 1000, ...

> Multiplying and dividing by 10, 100, 1000. ...
> involves moving digits to the left or right.
>
> $\times 10$ 3 1.7 5 → 3 1 7.5
> Move one place left.
>
> $\times 100$ 4 6.0 3 → 4 6 0 3.
> Move two places left.
>
> $\div 100$ 5 4 1.7 → 5.4 1 7
> Move two places right.

Do these in your head.

A1 (a) 4.2×10 (b) 53.1×100 (c) 10×0.46 (d) $58.3 \div 10$ (e) $29.4 \div 100$

A2 (a) 1.8×1000 (b) $3472 \div 10$ (c) 2.48×100 (d) $3951 \div 100$ (e) 0.052×10

B Multiplying by 20, 30, 200, ...

> 20 is 2×10.
> To multiply by 20, you can multiply by 2 and then by 10.
>
> 1.4×20
>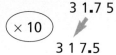
> $1.4 \xrightarrow{\times 2} 2.8 \xrightarrow{\times 10} 28$
>
> To multiply by 300, you can multiply by 3 and then by 100.
>
> 15×300
> $15 \xrightarrow{\times 3} 45 \xrightarrow{\times 100} 4500$

B1 (a) 13×20 (b) 23×30 (c) 114×200 (d) 1.5×300 (e) 21×400

B2 (a) 6×500 (b) 20×320 (c) 1.2×40 (d) 30×1.5 (e) 2.2×300

C $30 \times 40, 30 \times 400, ...$

Start with 3×4.	$3 \times$	$4 =$	**12**
From this you can work out 30×4.	$30 \times$	$4 =$	**120**
Then you can do 30×40, ...	$30 \times$	$40 =$	**1200**
... and 30×400.	$30 \times 400 =$		**12000**

C1 (a) 20×60 (b) 30×500 (c) 20×400 (d) 300×30 (e) 50×40

C2 (a) 30×600 (b) 700×200 (c) 20×900 (d) 60×60 (e) 300×30

C3 (a) 500×40 (b) 80×60 (c) 50×700 (d) 2000×40 (e) 60×5000

C4 Felt-tips cost 30p each.
Work out the cost, in pounds, of 200 felt-tips.

C5 Work out the cost, in pounds, of
(a) 80 rulers at 40p each   (b) 500 pencils at 20p each   (c) 400 pens at 60p each

D Place value

D1 In the number **23 654**, the figure **6** stands for 6 **hundreds**, or 600.
The figure **2** stands for 2 **ten thousands**, or 20 000.
(a) What does the figure 3 stand for?   (b) What does the figure 5 stand for?

D2 In the number **497 536,**
(a) What does the figure 4 stand for?   (b) What does the figure 9 stand for?

D3 In your head, work out
(a) $3518 + 100$ (b) $53\,763 - 1000$ (c) $42\,071 + 300$ (d) $146\,510 + 2000$
(e) $90\,384 - 100$ (f) $471\,593 + 2000$ (g) $90\,342 + 5000$ (h) $276\,540 - 2000$

D4 Before Jan went on holiday, her car's mileometer said $\boxed{5\ 7\ 6\ 2\ 4}$.
When she got back, it said $\boxed{5\ 9\ 6\ 2\ 4}$.
How many miles did Jan travel on holiday?

D5 St. Paul's Cathedral in London was built in 1711.
(a) In which year was it 200 years old?
(b) In which year will it be 2000 years old?
(c) In which year will it be 20 000 years old (if it lasts that long!)?

E Rounding to the nearest ten, hundred, ...

E1 The world's longest river is the Nile. It is 4132 miles long.
Round the number 4132

(a) to the nearest hundred   (b) to the nearest ten   (c) to the nearest thousand

E2 The distance from London to Wellington (New Zealand) is 11 682 miles.
Round the number 11 682 to the nearest

(a) thousand   (b) ten thousand   (c) hundred   (d) ten

E3 Round

(a) 46 023 to the nearest thousand   (b) 68 086 to the nearest hundred

(c) 647 254 to the nearest ten thousand   (d) 7 835 091 to the nearest million

F Rounding to one significant figure

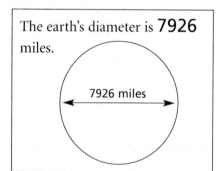

The earth's diameter is **7926** miles.

7926 miles

The highest place value in the number **7926** is thousands.

If we round to the nearest thousand, we get **8000**.

This is called rounding to **one significant figure**.

Examples of rounding to one significant figure

Number	Highest place value	Rounded to one significant figure
628	hundreds	600
28047	ten thousands	30000
6851	thousands	7000

F1 Round each of these numbers to one significant figure.

(a) 537   (b) 1742   (c) 26 410   (d) 2396   (e) 86 421

F2 Round each of these numbers to one significant figure.

(a) 7.2   (b) 8139   (c) 756   (d) 342 613   (e) 28 854

(f) 3096   (g) 441   (h) 48 572   (i) 5 873 441   (j) 620 711

*F3 Round 968 to one significant figure.

Ⓖ *Rough estimates*

This concert hall has 42 rows of seats.
There are 29 seats in each row.

The total number of seats is 42 × 29.

You can estimate the answer by **rounding the numbers
to one significant figure:**

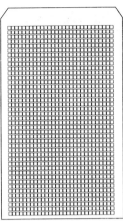

> 42 × 29
>
> Rough estimate: 40 × 30 = **1200**

G1 Find a rough estimate for each of these.

(a) 37 × 51   (b) 48 × 33   (c) 69 × 28   (d) 196 × 43   (e) 288 × 41

G2 A group of 57 people go on a coach trip.
Each person pays £32 for the trip.
Estimate how much money they pay altogether.

G3 A cable car carries 36 people each time it goes to the top of a mountain.
One day it made 53 trips to the top.
Estimate how many people it took to the top that day.

G4 Find a rough estimate for each of these.

(a) 71 × 78   (b) 62 × 418   (c) 286 × 411   (d) 83 × 592   (e) 731 × 391

Test yourself with these questions

Do all the questions in your head.

T1 (a) 40.5 × 10   (b) 100 × 2.6   (c) 0.68 × 100   (d) 316 ÷ 10   (e) 42.7 ÷ 100

T2 (a) 520 × 20   (b) 22 × 400   (c) 1.2 × 200   (d) 150 × 20   (e) 17 × 2000

T3 (a) 60 × 30   (b) 200 × 40   (c) 5000 × 80   (d) 400 × 90   (e) 600 × 700

T4 Round each of these numbers to one significant figure.

(a) 7641   (b) 32 957   (c) 887   (d) 1064   (e) 462 855

T5 Work out a rough estimate for each of these.

(a) 52 × 78   (b) 318 × 48   (c) 196 × 68   (d) 408 × 378   (e) 93 × 2754

T6 Grant does housework once a week for an elderly person.
He is paid £33 each time.
Roughly how much does he earn in 48 weeks?

Review 1

1 Work out the area of each of these shapes.

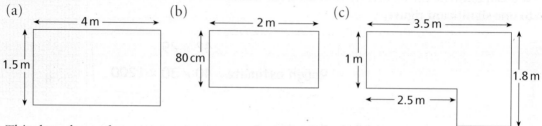

(a) 4 m 1.5 m

(b) 2 m 80 cm

(c) 3.5 m 1 m 2.5 m 1.8 m

2 This data shows the noon temperature and amount of rainfall in Barcelona and London each day in a week in July.

	Barcelona							London						
	M	Tu	W	Th	F	Sa	Su	M	Tu	W	Th	F	Sa	Su
Noon temp (°C)	23	24	30	32	28	26	26	18	16	25	28	17	19	17
Rainfall (mm)	0	0	4	0	3	6	4	0	6	2	7	8	12	0

(a) (i) Which city was hotter on Monday?   (ii) By how many degrees?

(b) On what day was the difference in rainfall between the two cities greatest?

(c) On the same scales, draw line graphs of the noon temperature in the two cities. Start the temperature (the vertical) scale at 10°C.

(d) On what day was the difference in temperature between the two cities greatest?

(e) Work out the mean noon temperature in (i) Barcelona (ii) London.

(f) Work out the range in the temperatures in each city for this week.

3 Work out the missing angles in each of these diagrams.   Not to scale

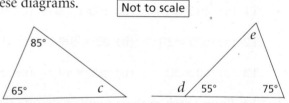

a 75°

b 125°

85° 65° c

e d 55° 75°

4 Copy and complete each of these.

(a)

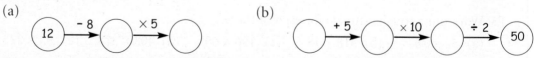

12 − 8 × 5

(b)

+ 5 × 10 ÷ 2 50

5 Draw an arrow diagram for each of these equations.
Reverse each diagram to solve the equation. Check your answers work.

(a) $4x + 1 = 29$ (b) $3p - 6 = 21$ (c) $\frac{w}{3} + 5 = 8$

Symmetrical shapes

This will help you revise

◆ the names of types of triangles, quadrilaterals and other polygons

◆ how to recognize the lines of symmetry of a shape, and describe rotational symmetry

You should also learn about

◆ the types of symmetry in common shapes

◆ how to complete shapes with given symmetry

A Describing shapes

This diagram shows a regular hexagon that has been split into two trapeziums.

Sheet P18 has some more regular hexagons.

Use the sheet to show how a hexagon can be split into:

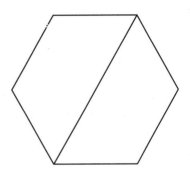

A Three rhombuses

B Six equilateral triangles

C Four trapeziums

D A kite and two isosceles triangles

E A rectangle and two isosceles triangles

F An equilateral triangle and three isosceles triangles

G An isosceles triangle and two trapeziums

A1 Here is a piece of a mosaic pattern. Describe the shaded shapes in as much detail as possible.

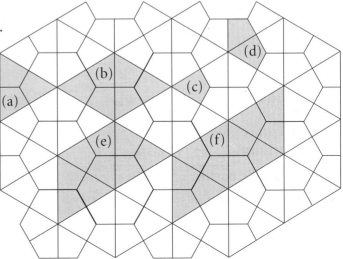

B Symmetrical triangles

There are two types of symmetry, **reflection** and **rotation.**

A shape with reflection symmetry has mirror lines which reflect one half of the shape exactly onto the other half.

A shape with rotation symmetry can be turned so that it fits on top of itself more than one way.
The **order** of rotation symmetry is the number of different positions a shape fits on top of itself.
We say that a shape with no rotation symmetry has order 1 as it only fits on top of itself in 1 way.

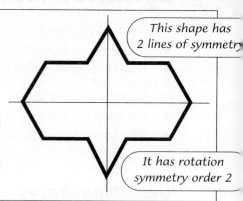

This shape has 2 lines of symmetry

It has rotation symmetry order 2

B1 This question is on sheet P20.

B2 This triangular grid has been shaded so that it has one line of symmetry and rotation symmetry order 1.

Describe the symmetry of these shaded triangular grids.

(a)   (b)   (c) 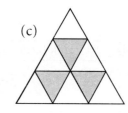 (d)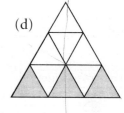

(e) 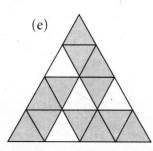 (f)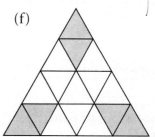

B3 This question is on sheet P19.

B4 For each of these triangles, say
  (i) what type of triangle it is
  (ii) the number of lines of symmetry it has
  (iii) the order of rotation symmetry it has

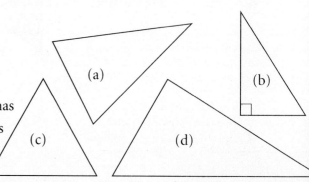

C *Polygon symmetry*

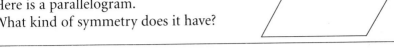

> Here is a parallelogram.
> What kind of symmetry does it have?

C1 (a) Draw a rectangle and show any lines of symmetry it has.

(b) What order of rotation symmetry does a rectangle have?

(c) Describe the symmetry of a square.

C2 Here is a trapezium.

(a) Describe the symmetry of this trapezium.

(b) Can you draw another trapezium which has no reflection symmetry?

C3 Draw some different rhombuses.
What can you say about the symmetry of a rhombus?

C4 Draw some different kites.
What can you say about the symmetry of a kite?

C5 Draw a quadrilateral which has no symmetry at all.

C6 Here are some regular polygons.

(a) Copy and complete this table:

Polygon	No. of sides	Lines of symmetry	Order of rotation symmetry
Equilateral triangle	3	3	3
Square	4		
Regular pentagon	5		
Regular hexagon			
Regular nonagon			

Nonogon

Pentagon   Hexagon

(b) What symmetry would a regular icosagon (20 sides) have?

What am I?

What shapes are being described?

> *I have three sides.*
> *I have one line of symmetry.*
> *I have no rotation symmetry*

> *I have four sides, none of which are parallel.*
> *I have one line of symmetry.*
> *I have no rotation symmetry.*

Make some up of your own.
Try them on a friend.

D *Getting coordinated*

D1 All the shapes in this diagram are
one half of a quadrilateral.
Each one has line M as a
line of symmetry.

For each quadrilateral:

(i) On sheet P21 draw in the rest of
the shape after reflection in line M.

(ii) Give the coordinates of any points
needed to complete the shape.

(iii) Write down the name of the
quadrilateral.

D2 Use the coordinate grid on sheet P21
to do the following.

Draw a line going from (6, 0) to (6, 12).

For each of A, B and C below:

- Plot the points. The points make
half of a shape which has symmetry in the line you have drawn.

- Complete the shape and describe it

A (6, 12) (9, 9) (6, 10)   **B** (6, 9) (8, 8) (8, 6) (6, 5)   **C** (6, 4) (9, 3) (6, 0)

D3 This diagram shows half of a shape which has
rotation symmetry order 2 around centre (0, 0).

(a) What new coordinate completes the shape?

(b) What is the name of this shape?

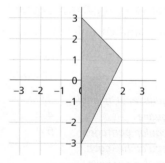

D4 Using the same size grid as D3, plot each of these sets of points.
For each set, add further points to make a shape
with rotation symmetry order 2 around centre (0,0).

(a) (2, 0) (2, 3) (⁻2, 0)   (b) (3, 0) (0, 2) (⁻3, 0)   (c) (1, 0) (3, 3) (1, 3) (⁻1, 0)

Name each of the shapes.

D5 The points below are part of shapes with rotational
symmetry **order 4** around centre (0, 0).

Plot these on a grid as in D3 and complete the shape.

(a) (3, 0) (0, ⁻3)   (b) (0, 2) (⁻3, 3) (⁻2, 0)

D6 (a) Draw a grid going from ⁻4 to 4 on both axes.

(b) Plot the points (4, 0) (4, 2) (2, 4) (0, 4).

(c) Complete the shape so that it has 4 lines of symmetry.

(d) What order of rotational symmetry does this shape have?

Test yourself with these questions

T1 Here are 4 patterns in equilateral triangles

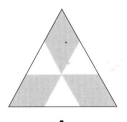 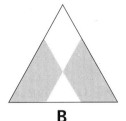 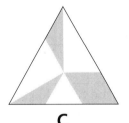 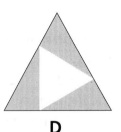

A   B   C   D

(a) Which pattern has reflection symmetry but no rotation symmetry?

(b) Which pattern has rotation symmetry but no reflection symmetry?

(c) Which pattern has reflection symmetry and rotation symmetry?

T2 Here are 4 quadrilaterals.

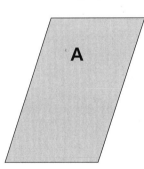 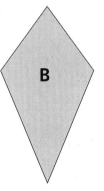 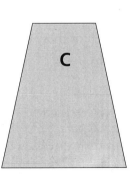 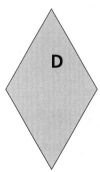

A   B   C   D

(a) Give the special names for each of these shapes.

(b) How many lines of symmetry does shape B have?

(c) How many lines of symmetry does shape A have.

(d) Which of these shapes has rotation symmetry order 2?

(e) Which of these shapes has rotation and reflection symmetry?

7 Working with formulas

You should know that
♦ if *a* stands for a number, we can write $4 \times a$ as $4a$.
♦ the expression $4a + 6$ means 'multiply *a* by 4, then add 6'.
♦ the expression $3(b + 5)$ means 'add 5 to *b*, then multiply by 3'.

This work will help you learn how to
♦ find a formula or expression describing a pattern.
♦ draw a graph from a pattern formula.
♦ extend a pattern graph and use it for predictions.
♦ form equations from patterns and use them to solve problems.

A Expression review

Examples

Find the value of $2p$ when $p = 4$.
$2p = 2 \times 4 = 8$

Find the value of $q + 6$ when $q = 3$.
$q + 6 = 3 + 6 = 9$

Find the value of $3s + 2$ when $s = 5$.
$3s + 2 = 3 \times 5 + 2$ $= 15 + 2 = 17$

Find the value of $2(r + 1)$ when $r = 4$.
$2(r + 1) = 2 \times (4 + 1)$ $= 2 \times 5 = 10$

A1 Work out the value of each of these when $z = 6$.
  (a) $z + 4$ (b) $5z$ (c) $z - 4$ (d) $2z$

A2 What is the value of each of these expressions when $f = 5$?
  (a) $4f$ (b) $f + 4$ (c) $f - 4$ (d) $4 + f$

A3 Work out each of these when $g = 4$.
  (a) $2g + 1$ (b) $2(g + 1)$ (c) $2(1 + g)$ (d) $2 + g$

A4 Work out the value of the expression $4(m + 2)$ when
  (a) $m = 3$ (b) $m = 5$ (c) $m = \frac{1}{2}$ (d) $m = 0$

A5 Work out
  (a) $10 - h$ when $h = 3$ (b) $4(j + 3)$ when $j = 1$ (c) $3k + 7$ when $k = 2$

A6 When $a = 5$, which is bigger, $2a + 1$ or $2(a + 1)$?

B Know your tables

B1 *Busby's Banquets* organise meals.
They set out square tables in rows.

One of these tables needs 4 chairs.

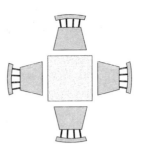

For two tables they need 6 chairs.

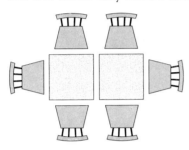

And for three tables they need 8 chairs.

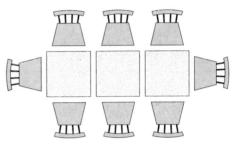

(a) How many chairs do Busby's need for 4 square tables?

(b) How many do they need for 10 tables?

(c) How many do they need at 100 tables?

(d) Copy and complete this (mathematical!) table.

Number of tables	1	2	3	4	5	6	10	100
Number of chairs	4	6	8					

(e) Which of these is correct for the rule connecting
the number of square tables and the number of chairs?

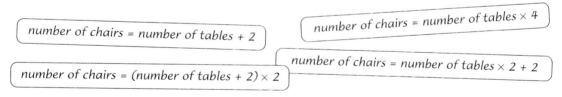

number of chairs = number of tables + 2

number of chairs = number of tables × 4

number of chairs = (number of tables + 2) × 2

number of chairs = number of tables × 2 + 2

(f) Suppose *t* stands for the number of tables
and *c* stands for the number of chairs.
Which of these rules is correct?

$c = t + 2$ $c = 2(t + 2)$ $c = 2t + 2$ $c = 4t$

B2 *Busby's* also use rectangular tables.
Sometimes they set out the
rectangular tables like this.

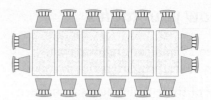

First they put out two chairs
with every table....

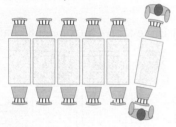

...then they put the four extra chairs
at the ends.

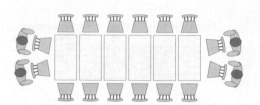

(a) How many chairs do Busby's need when
they use 10 rectangular tables set out like this?

(b) How many do they need at 20 tables?

(c) For tables set out like this, copy and complete:

Number of tables (t)	1	2	3	4	5	6	10	100
Number of chairs (c)								

(d) Here are some rules written in words.
Which of the rules is correct connecting
the *number of tables* and the *number of chairs*?

number of chairs = (number of tables + 4) × 2

number of chairs = number of tables × 6

number of chairs = number of tables × 2 + 4

number of chairs = number of tables + 2

(e) Suppose *t* stands for the *number of tables*
and *c* stands for the *number of chairs*.

Look at these four formulas connecting *c* and *t*.

$c = t + 2$ $c = 2(t + 4)$ $c = 2t + 4$ $c = 6t$

A **formula** is just
a rule using letters.

Which of the formulas is correct?

B3 Sometimes *Busby's* arrange their rectangular tables in a line.

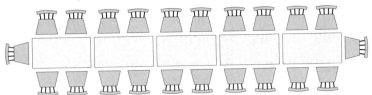

(a) If they use 10 tables in a line, how many chairs do they need?

(b) If they use 100 tables in a line, how many chairs do they need?

(c) Write a rule in words telling you the number of chairs you need
when you know the *number of tables*.

Start your rule like this: *number of chairs = ...*

(d) Which of these formulas tells you
the number of chairs (*c*) when you
know the number of tables (*t*)?

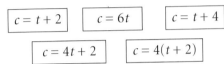

$c = t + 2$ $c = 6t$ $c = t + 4$

$c = 4t + 2$ $c = 4(t + 2)$

B4 Here is another arrangement
using larger tables.

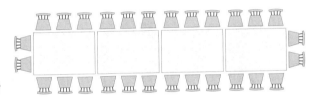

(a) How many chairs does this
arrangement need for 100 tables?

(b) Write a rule in words telling you the *number of chairs* you need
when you know the *number of tables*.

(c) Write your rule as a formula, using letters.
Use *t* to stand for the *number of tables*
and *c* to stand for the *number of chairs*.

B5 This arrangement uses triangular tables.

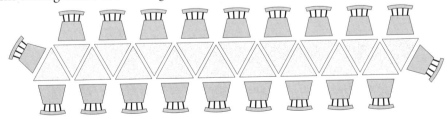

(a) For this triangular arrangement, work out a rule in words telling you
the *number of chairs* you need when you know the *number of tables*.

(b) Write your rule as a formula, where *t* stands for the *number of tables*
and *c* stands for the *number of chairs*.

C *Pendants*

C1 James makes pendants in gold.
He links together small gold bars to make each pendant.

He makes different types of pendant.
These are 'SuperDrop' pendants.

SuperDrops ...

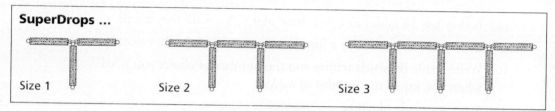

Size 1   Size 2   Size 3

(a) How many gold bars are there in the size 1 *SuperDrop?*

(b) How many gold bars are there in (i) a size 2   (ii) a size 3?

(c) How many **extra** bars do you add to a
size 3 *SuperDrop* to make a size 4?

(d) Without sketching, work out the number of gold bars in

   (i) a size 10 *SuperDrop*   (ii) a size 20 *SuperDrop.*

(e) Copy and complete this table for the *SuperDrop* pendants.

SuperDrop size (*n*)	1	2	3	4	5	6	10	20
Number of bars (*g*)								

(f) Which of these rules is correct for the *SuperDrops?*
   A   *number of gold bars = size number × 3*
   B   *number of gold bars = size number × 2 + 1*
   C   *number of gold bars = size number + 2*
   D   *number of gold bars = (size number + 1) × 2*

(g) Write a formula using letters for the number of gold bars in the *SuperDrops.*
Use *g* to stand for the *number of gold bars* and
n to stand for the size number of the *SuperDrop.*

C2 James also makes 'SuperSquare' pendants.
Here is a size 3 and a size 5 SuperSquare.

SuperSquares ...

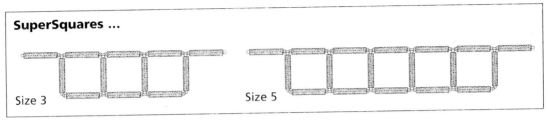

Size 3   Size 5

To make SuperSquare pendants, James first
makes up sets of bars in threes, like this:

Then, if he wants a size 4 SuperSquare,
he first joins together 4 of his sets.

Then he adds the extra bars
he needs to complete the pendant.

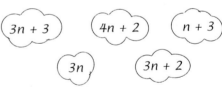

(a) How many gold bars does James use in a size 4 SuperSquare?

(b) How many gold bars are in a size 10 SuperSquare?

(c) If James made a size 100 SuperSquare, how many bars would be need?

(d) Explain how you can work out the number of gold bars
needed when you know the size number.

(e) Choose one of the expressions on the right
to complete the sentence:

*If the size number of a SuperSquare is n
then the number of gold bars in it is...*

$3n + 3$ $4n + 2$ $n + 3$

$3n$ $3n + 2$

C3 These are two of James's *Glissando* pendants.
On the left is a size 2; on the right is a size 4.

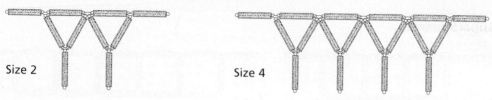

Size 2 Size 4

Which of these expressions tells you the number of gold bars
in a size *n* Glissando pendant?

| $4n$ | $4n - 2$ | $4n + 2$ | $6n$ | $4(n + 2)$ |

C4 Below are three more of James's pendant designs.
On the right are some expressions for
the number of gold bars in a size *n* pendant.

| $3n + 1$ | $6n + 2$ | $5n + 3$ |

Which expression goes with which design?

The Triangular ...

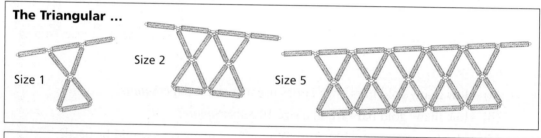

Size 1   Size 2   Size 5

The Simple ...

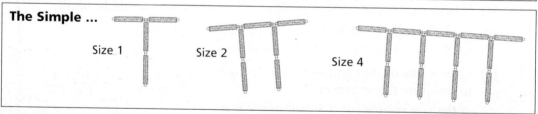

Size 1   Size 2   Size 4

The Tri-square ...

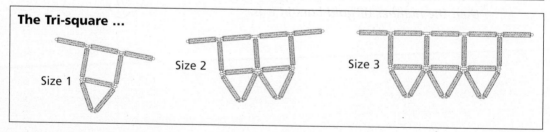

Size 1   Size 2   Size 3

C5 In James's *Expressive* pendant there are $3n + 2$ bars in a size *n* pendant.

(a) How many bars are there in the size 1 pendant?

(b) How many are there in the size 2 pendant?

(c) Draw a sketch of what you think James's size 1 and
size 2 *Expressive* pendants might look like.

D Graphs

D1 This is one of James's *Tribar* pendants. It is a size 5 *Tribar* pendant.

Size 5

A size *n Tribar* pendant is made from $3n + 4$ gold bars.

(a) Check that this expression is correct for the size 5 pendant.

(b) Use the expression $3n + 4$ to work out the number of
gold bars in a size 2 *Tribar* pendant.
Draw a sketch to check your answer.

(c) Use the expression to copy and complete this table.

Size of Tribar (*n*)	1	2	3	4	5
Number of gold bars (*g*)					19

D2 James uses a graph to show how
many bars are in each size of *Tribar*.

The point (5, 19) is plotted here.
It shows that when *n* is 5, *g* is 19.

It shows that a size 5 *Tribar* uses 19 gold bars.

(a) Copy the graph on the right
onto squared paper.
Make the across axis go from 0 to 6
and the up axis go from 0 to 22.

Label the axes and plot the point (5, 19).

(b) From your table in question 1, plot
crosses for each size of *Tribar*.

(c) What do you notice about the points
that you have plotted?

(d) Join the points.
With a ruler, extend your line
to the edges of the graph.

(e) When *n* is 6, what is *g* on your line?

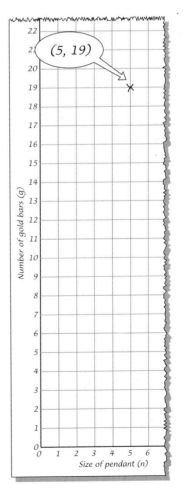

D3 In James's *Excellence* design there are
$2n + 2$ gold bars in the size n pendant.

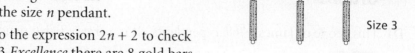

Size 3

(a) Substitute 3 into the expression $2n + 2$ to check
that in the size 3 *Excellence* there are 8 gold bars.

(b) How many gold bars are there in the size 4 *Excellence*?

(c) How many gold bars are there in size 5?

(d) Copy and complete this table for the *Excellence* pendants.

Size of pendant (n)	1	2	3	4	5
Number of gold bars (g)			8		

(e) On squared paper, draw axes going from 0 to 8 across
and from 0 to 20 up.
Label the axes like you did in question 1.

(f) Plot points for the table above on your graph.
For example, when $n = 3$ you can see that $g = 8$.
So plot a point at $(3, 8)$.

(g) Join your points with a line, and extend it upwards.

(h) Use your extended line to find out what g is when $n = 6$.

(i) Use the graph to find out how many gold bars there are
in a size 7 *Excellence* pendant.

D4 James also makes necklaces from pearls.
This is one of his *Lustrous* necklaces.
It is a size 4 - it has 4 groups of three pearls.
Each *Lustrous* necklace has one extra pearl at each end.

Size 4

(a) Copy and complete this table for *Lustrous* necklaces.

Size of necklace (n)	2	3	4	5	6
Number of pearls (p)			14		

(b) Which of these expressions is correct for the
number of pearls (p) in a size n necklace?

$\boxed{3n + 2}$ $\boxed{3n + 1}$ $\boxed{4n}$

(c) On squared paper, draw axes going from 0 to 6 across
and from 0 to 24 up.
Label the across axis *Size of necklace (n)* and the up axis *Number of pearls (p)*.

(d) Plot points for the table above on your graph and
join them with a straight line.

(e) Extend your line to find out how many pearls there are
in a size 1 *Lustrous* necklace. Draw a sketch to check your answer.

E Equations

Here are two of James's *Janglie* necklaces.

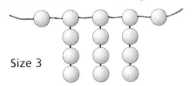

Size 3   Size 5

A size 3 *Janglie* has 4 × 3 + 2 pearls in it.
A size 5 *Janglie* has 4 × 5 + 2 pearls in it.

A size *n Janglie* will have 4 × *n* + 2 or 4*n* + 2 pearls in it.

A customer wants a *Janglie* with 150 pearls in it!
Which size *Janglie* should James make?

We can solve this problem like this.

The number of pearls in a size *n Janglie* is 4*n* + 2.
We want to find when the number of pearls is 150.

So we want to find when 4*n* + 2 is 150.

We can write the equation 4*n* + 2 = 150.
Now we can solve the equation using arrow diagrams.

- Draw an arrow diagram
  for the equation.

- Reverse the arrow diagram
  to find the value of *n*.

- Check that your value of *n*
  works in the original problem.

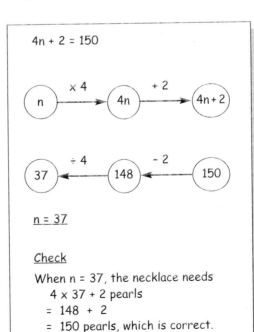

4n + 2 = 150

n $\xrightarrow{\times 4}$ 4n $\xrightarrow{+ 2}$ 4n + 2

37 $\xleftarrow{\div 4}$ 148 $\xleftarrow{- 2}$ 150

n = 37

Check

When n = 37, the necklace needs
    4 × 37 + 2 pearls
  = 148 + 2
  = 150 pearls, which is correct.

E1 A size *n Janglie* necklace has $4n + 2$ pearls in it.
One size of *Janglie* has 70 pearls in it.

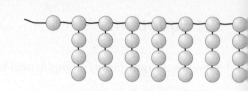

Copy and complete this working to work out
which size *Janglie* it is.

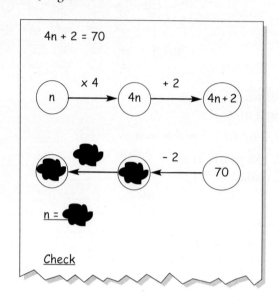

E2 A customer orders a *Janglie* necklace with 94 pearls.

Work out which size *Janglie* it is.
Show your working like in question D1.

E3 A size *n Tribar* pendant is made
from $3n + 4$ gold bars.

Size 5

James makes a *Tribar* using 55 gold bars.

Copy and complete this working
to find out what size the *Tribar* is.

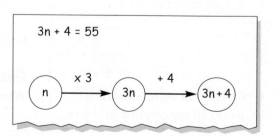

E4 A size *n Excellence* pendant is made from $2n + 2$ gold bars.

Size 3

One *Excellence* pendant is made from 50 gold bars.

Work out what size it is.
Show all your working and check your answer.

E5 Below are three sizes of James's *DeLuxe* necklace.

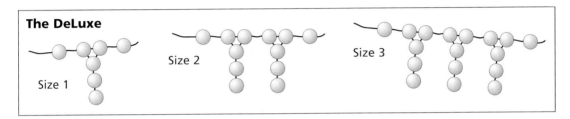

The DeLuxe

Size 1

Size 2

Size 3

(a) Which of the expressions on the right tells you the number of pearls in a size *n DeLuxe* necklace?

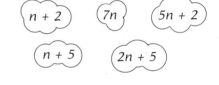

$n + 2$ $7n$ $5n + 2$

$n + 5$ $2n + 5$

(b) A customer wants a *DeLuxe* necklace made from 122 pearls.
Work out what size it is.

Show all your working and check your answer.

*E6 James *Supreme* is his most expensive type of pearl necklace.
Here are three different sizes of *Supreme*.

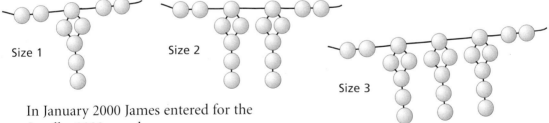

Size 1

Size 2

Size 3

In January 2000 James entered for the *Jeweller 2000* award.

His entry was a *Supreme* necklace made from exactly 400 pearls!

What size was the necklace?

Test yourself with these questions

T1 This picture shows a table arrangement with a row of 3 tables

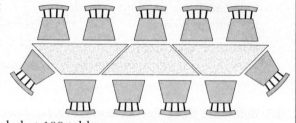

(a) How many chairs are there in this row of 3 tables?

(b) How many chairs will there be in a row of 4 tables?

(c) Work out the number of chairs needed at 100 tables set out in a row like this.

(d) Copy and complete for the arrangement.

Number of tables	1	2	3	4	100
Number of chairs					

(e) Which of these formulas tells you the number of chairs (c) when you know the number of tables (t)?

$c = 3t + 2$	$c = 2t + 3$	$c = 5t$	$c = t + 2$	$c = 2t - 1$

T2 (a) On squared paper, draw axes going from 0 to 6 across and from 0 to 20 up.
Label the across axis *number of tables* (*t*)
and the up axis *number of chairs* (*c*).

(b) From your table in question T1(d),
plot crosses showing the number of chairs for 1, 2, 3 and 4 tables.

(c) Join your points with a line.

(d) Extend your line to find c when *t* is 6.

T3 Here are three sizes of *Black beauty* necklaces. They are made from black pearls.

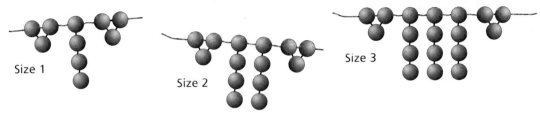

Size 1

Size 2

Size 3

(a) Which of these expressions tells you
the number of black pearls
in a size *n* *Black beauty* necklace?

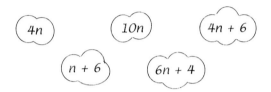

$4n$ $10n$ $4n + 6$

$n + 6$ $6n + 4$

One size of *Black beauty* necklace
uses 90 black pearls.

(b) Write down an equation that tells you this.

(c) Use arrow diagrams to work out which size necklace it is.

(d) Check that your answer is correct.

8 Experiments

This work should help you to design an experiment to answer a question and to write a report on it.

You should learn to make use of finding means, medians, modes, ranges and frequency tables and charts to help you write your report.

A Memory experiments

Thanks for the memory

Which do people remember best, words, pictures or numbers?

heather	school
lamp	sky
hate	spoon
necklace	birthday
hair	leaf

Here are some descriptions of how some pupils carried out a memory experiment. Do you think they are good methods? Give your reasons.

We used 10 words to test the memory of our class.
We asked the class next door to do a memory test using 10 pictures and another class to use 10 numbers.
We then compared the results from the three classes.

We have roughly the same number of boys as girls in our class, so we got the boys to remember words and the girls pictures.
The boys had 10 words to remember.
The girls had 15 pictures as we thought pictures were easier.
We showed them for 30 seconds and we had 1 minute to write down as many as we could remember from our lists.

Describe how you might carry out an experiment to test these questions:

- Can people remember a list of words better if there is music in the background?
- Students cannot do a standing jump as high after eating their lunch.
- The hand that people write with is stronger than their other hand.

B Looking at results

Twenty five students in a class took part in a memory experiment.
Here are the results of the number of words they remembered out of 10.

Words: 8, 5, 5, 7, 8, 10, 9, 10, 9, 8, 9, 10, 9, 7, 8, 10, 7, 7, 8, 9, 10, 9, 9, 7, 8

A dotplot is a useful way of showing the results.

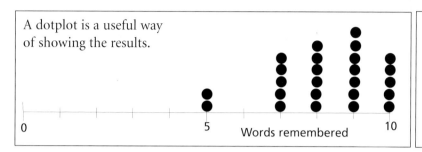

The **mode** or **modal** value is the one with the highest frequency.

The modal number of words remembered in the class is 9.

A frequency table is useful for storing the results.

Words	Tally	Frequency
5	/ /	2
6		0
7	////	5
8	//// /	6
9	//// //	7
10	////	5
	Total	25

A bar chart of these results shows the pattern more clearly.

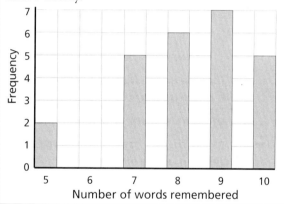

The **median** is the middle number when they are put in order.
The **range** is the difference between the largest and smallest number.

Here are the number of words remembered by the class in order.

Words: 5, 5, 7, 7, 7, 7, 7, 8, 8, 8, 8, 8, 8, 9, 9, 9, 9, 9, 9, 9, 10, 10, 10, 10, 10

The median is 8 words.
The range is 10 – 5 = 5 words

Sometimes the **mean** is used instead of the median.

This is found by adding up all the results and dividing by the number of results there are.

For the number of words remembered by the class:

Total = 5+5+7+7+7+7+7+8+8+8+8+8+8+9+9+9+9+9+9+9+10+10+10+10+10 = 206

Mean = 206 ÷ 25 = 8.24 words

C Writing a report

When you write a report on your experiments here are some useful tips.

- State clearly the question you wanted to answer.

> **Remembering words, pictures and numbers**
>
> *We wanted to see if there was any difference between how good young people are at remembering words, pictures and numbers*

- Describe carefully how you carried out your investigation and what you did to make sure it was done fairly.

> *We chose one class at random from each year from Year 7 to Year 13 to take part.*
>
> *We made three charts which showed*
>
> - *10 words which had no connection with each other*
> - *10 pictures of simple objects*
> - *10 numbers between 10 and 99*
>
> *We showed each class the 10 words for 30 seconds and then gave them 1 minute to write down as many as they could remember. The order didn't matter.*
>
> *We then did the same with the pictures and the numbers.*
>
> *We asked them to swap papers to mark them and everyone wrote their 3 scores on a slip of paper.*

- When drawing diagrams and calculating values such as the mean, only use those which actually help you to answer your question.

- When writing about what you find only make statements which your results clearly show are true.

> *The mean and the median are highest for remembering pictures so we think that pictures are the easiest to remember. Pictures also had the highest range which shows that the results were more spread out.*

- Make some suggestions as to how you could improve your experiment or carry out more research.

> *We would like to try this experiment again using 20 words, pictures and numbers as quite a few people got them all right with just 10.*

These experiments have some questions you could try to answer yourself.
Design your own experiment to test one of these questions or one of your own.

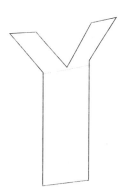

Helicopter seeds

The sycamore tree has seeds with wings which
make it fall more slowly to earth - but has nature
come up with the best design?

- Cut a strip of card 5 cm wide and 20 cm long.
  Cut a a slit 2 cm long from the top and bend back
  the wings.
- Drop your 'helicopter' from a safe high place and time
  how long it takes to fall to earth. Repeat a few times.
- Does the length of the slit affect how long the helicopter
  takes to fall?
- Does the length and width of the strip affect how long it
  takes to fall?
- Does putting blu-tack on the helicopter affect the time?

Word lengths

- Do some newspapers use shorter words than others?
- Do books or magazines for teenagers use shorter words than adult books?
- Do different authors use words of different lengths?

9 Into the crowd

You will revise
◆ how to read and plot points on a graph.

You will also learn
◆ how to describe what is happening on a graph.
◆ how to sketch a graph for a real-life situation.

A Noise

Noise probe call City Mail

Residents near City's ground called for action against noise on match days. They recorded the noise at last Saturday's match against Ribchester Rovers, saying it was far above permitted levels.

Blonde mother of six Mrs Betty Bowland, City resident for 15 years, said 'It's not me I worry about, it's all us with young kids. Can't sleep at all, they can't, on match days'

Last Saturday City turned out 25,000 fans against Ribchester Rovers 10,000. It was a lively crowd, said our reporter Tom Drivel, and the noise was about average for a Saturday game.

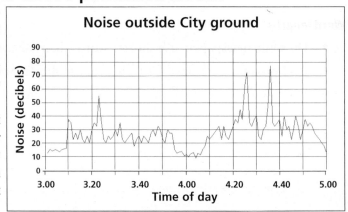

Noise outside City ground

A1 Look at the graph of the noise at the football match.

(a) At about what time do you think the match actually started?
(It was not 3.00 o'clock.)

(b) Roughly when did half-time begin?

(c) About what time did the match end?

A2 (a) How many goals do you think were scored?

(b) City had 25 000 fans at the match; Ribchester Rovers had 10 000.
What do you think the score was at the end of the match?

A3 Noise is regularly monitored at rock concerts.
Here is a noise chart and a newspaper cutting about a rock concert.

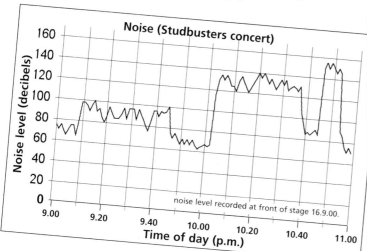

Never have the *Studbusters* played better. Last night's concert at Heathcote Park was just brilliant. A noisy and energetic crowd gave them a huge welcome and just kept on cheering. The quiet ballad 'Down mine' was followed by the ear-bending 'Deep fruit' - f a n t a s t i c ! In the first half, the support band *Stargaggle* were a bit quiet, but OK. All told an amazing night.

Read the newspaper cutting carefully.
Use the cutting and the noise chart to answer these questions.

(a) About what time do you think *Stargaggle* came on?

(b) There was an interval in the concert.
Roughly how long did it last?

(c) What time did the *Studbusters* start playing?

(d) Between what times did the *Studbusters* play 'Down mine'?

(e) 'Deep fruit' was earbending. When?

(f) About when did *Studbusters* go off?

(g) Health and Safety regulations state that the noise level at a concert
must not exceed 140dB at the front of the stage.
Was this level exceeded at the concert? If so, when?

A4 The noise in a playground changes during the day.
When everyone is in lessons it is quiet.
At other times it is noisier.

On squared paper, draw axes like these.

Sketch the noise level in your school
playground during the day.

Don't worry about decibels!
Just draw a sketch.

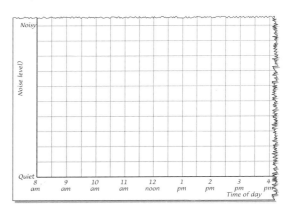

B Workout

Ellie works out at a gym.
She has a heart monitor that records her pulse rate every 10 seconds.

She switches the monitor on before she does any activity.

Here is a print-out and graph of her pulse rate
that she got when using a rowing machine.

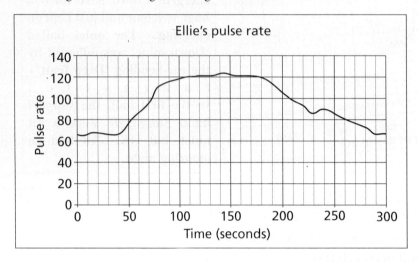

Ellie's pulse rate

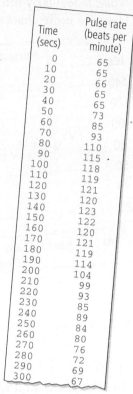

Time (secs)	Pulse rate (beats per minute)
0	65
10	65
20	66
30	65
40	65
50	73
60	85
70	93
80	110
90	115
100	118
110	119
120	121
130	120
140	123
150	122
160	120
170	121
180	119
190	114
200	104
210	99
220	93
230	85
240	89
250	84
260	80
270	76
280	72
290	69
300	67

Look carefully at the graph of Ellie's pulse rate.
She switched the machine on when the time was 0.
She waited a bit, then started rowing hard, and then stopped.

B1 (a) About how long did Ellie wait before starting rowing?

(b) What was the time on the graph when she stopped rowing?

(c) For about how long was she rowing?

(d) Roughly how long did it take Ellie's pulse
to get back to normal?

B2 (a) The maximum pulse rate (p) for a person aged n years
can be worked out using the formula $p = 220 - n$
Ellie is aged 50.
What is her maximum pulse rate?

(b) When training hard, your pulse rate should get
up to 80% of your maximum pulse rate.
Do you think Ellie is training hard enough?
Explain your reasons.

B3 This question is on sheet P22.

C *Temperature*

C1 The graph shows the temperature inside a new fridge.
The temperature was taken every minute over a two-hour period.

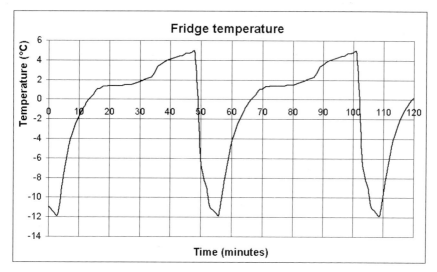

The fridge has a motor which cools down the inside.
The motor is switched on and off by a thermostat.

(a) What happens to the temperature in a fridge when the motor is running?

(b) At what temperature does the thermostat switch the motor on?

(c) What happens to the temperature when the motor is not running?

(d) At what temperature does the thermostat switch the motor off?

(e) For about how long does the motor run each time
it is switched on?

C2 This graph shows the temperature in a greenhouse during 24 hours in Summer.

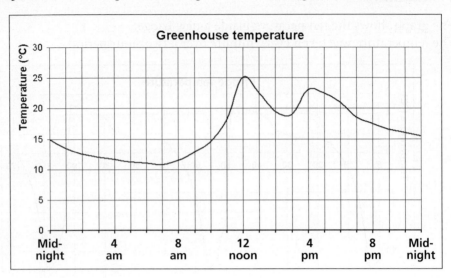

The temperature in a greenhouse falls during the night, and rises during the day. There are windows in this greenhouse to help keep the temperature down when it gets too hot.

(a) At roughly what time in the morning does the temperature in the greenhouse start to go up?

(b) About when during the day is the temperature going up fastest?

(c) About when is it going down fastest?

(d) Because it was getting too hot, the gardener opened a window in the greenhouse. Later she closed it again

   (i) About what time do you think she opened the window?

   (ii) Roughly when did she close it?

(e) What was the highest temperature in the greenhouse during the day?

(f) What was the lowest temperature in this 24 hours?

C3

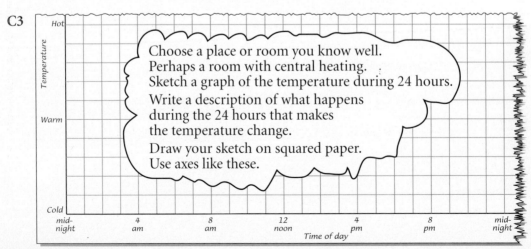

Choose a place or room you know well.
Perhaps a room with central heating.
Sketch a graph of the temperature during 24 hours.
Write a description of what happens during the 24 hours that makes the temperature change.
Draw your sketch on squared paper.
Use axes like these.

Test yourself with these questions

T1 This graph shows the number of people in a shopping centre one day near Christmas.

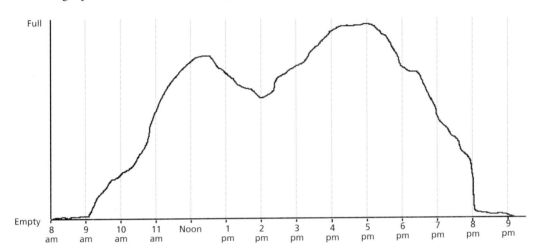

(a) What time do you think the shopping centre opened?

(b) What time do you think it closed?

(c) At roughly what time were there most people in the centre?

(d) At 1 p.m., was the centre empty, fairly empty, fairly full or full?

(e) Between noon and 6 p.m., when was it least full?

T2 This is part of the diary of Abir, who works in the shopping centre.
On squared paper, sketch a graph for Abir's day.

Number your across axis like in question T1.
Label your up axis *Cold* at the bottom and *Hot* at the top.

> *Got to work about 8 a.m. - it was really cold in the centre.*
>
> *The heating didn't come on until 10, and it only got warm by noon.*
>
> *By about 1 p.m. it was quite hot - and by 2 p.m. it was so hot they put the air-conditioning on to cool off a bit.*
>
> *At 4 p.m. we complained because it was now too cold! So they put the heating back on. But the heating broke down at 6 p.m. and by the time I left at half past 7 it was freezing again.*
>
> *Let's just hope they get it right tomorrow!*

10 Made to measure

This unit will help you practise changing between different metric measures such as metres and centimetres.

You will also learn about

♦ changing between metric measurements where kilo- and milli- are used

♦ changing between some imperial and metric measurements such as miles and kilometres, and pounds and kilograms.

A Metric lengths

Building materials such as screws and nails usually have their lengths given in millimetres.

This nail is 45 mm or 4.5 cm long.

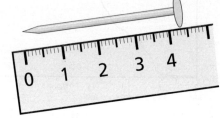

A1 Measure the lengths of these nails.
Write down their measurements in mm and cm.

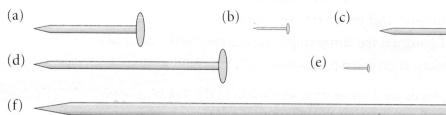

(a)

(b)

(c)

(d)

(e)

(f)

A2 Spiders are often measured by how wide their legs spread. Copy and complete this table showing the legspans of some spiders.

Spider	Span (mm)	Span (cm)
Bird-eating Spider	250 mm	
Tarantula		24 cm
Raft Spider (UK)	145 mm	
House Spider (UK)		7.5 cm
Wolf Spider (UK)	17 mm	
Money Spider (UK)	3 mm	

A3 Change the lengths of these snakes into centimetres.

Python 6 m   Anaconda 8.5 m   Grass Snake 1.25 m   Adder 0.75 m

A4 Change the wingspans of these bats into metres.

Fruit Bat   170 cm   Mouse-eared Bat (UK)   45 cm
Pipestrelle Bat (UK)   25 cm   Kitti's Hog-nosed Bat   9 cm

B Thousands of them

Using *kilo-* in front of a measure means a thousand of them.

A **kilo**metre is a thousand metres

A **kilogram** is a thousand grams

More or less	**What's in a gram**
Make a list of places in and around your school which are 'more' or 'less' than 1 kilometre away from your classroom. Check with a map.	How many pins weigh 1 gram? How much does a sheet of paper weigh? How many pins or sheets of paper make a kilogram? Can you find a single object which weighs 1 g?

B1 How many metres are there in each of these?

(a) 5 km   (b) 2.5 km   (c) 10 km   (d) 15.4 km

(e) 200 km   (f) 9.3 km   (g) 0.6 km   (h) 0.25 km

(i) a half of a kilometre   (j) three-quarters of a kilometre

B2 How many kilometres is each of these?

(a) 5000 m   (b) 20 000 m   (c) 100 000 m   (d) 1500 m

(e) 5800 m   (f) 500 m   (g) 100 m   (h) 750 m

B3 *Wholesome Catering Company* are making a large batch of Banana Cake. Here are the ingredients:

Copy the list but change all the amounts in grams to kilograms.

Banana Cake (makes 100 slices)
4500 g ripe bananas (mashed)
500 g chopped nuts
1000 g soya margarine
1250 g raisins
750 g rolled oats
1500 g wholewheat flour

B4 How many grams are there in each of these?

(a) 4 kg   (b) 2.5 kg   (c) 0.4 kg   (d) 0.75 kg

(e) a half of a kilogram   (f) a quarter of a kilogram

B5 How many of each of these packets would be needed to make 1 kg?

(a) 500 g   (b) 250 g   (c) 100 g   (d) 200 g

(e) 50 g   (f) 20 g   (g)  125 g   (h) 10 g

C *Thousands of pieces*

Using *milli* - in front of a measure means a thousandth of it.

1 . 2 5 0

1250 mm = 1.25 m

> A millimetre (mm) is one thousandth of a metre. There are 1000 milli**metres** in a metre

> A millilitre (ml) is one thousandth of a litre. There are 1000 milli**litres** in a litre

0 . 0 7 5

75 *ml* = 0.075 *l*

C1 Write these measurements in metres.

(a) 2000 mm   (b) 10000 mm   (c) 1500 mm   (d) 1695 mm

(e) 500 mm   (f) 750 mm   (g) 50 mm   (h) 10 mm

C2 How many millimetres are there in each of these?

(a) 5 m   (b) 50 m   (c) 2.5 m   (d) 5.5 m

(e) 0.6 m   (f) 0.25 m   (g) 4.75 m   (h) 0.065 m

C3 These kitchen units all have their units given in millimetres. Sketch the diagrams and change the measurements to metres

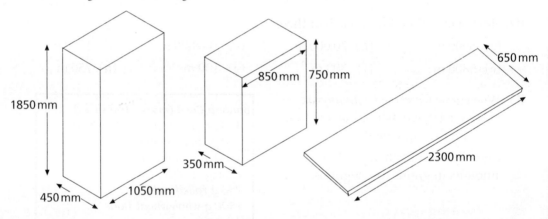

1850 mm   450 mm   1050 mm

850 mm   750 mm   350 mm

650 mm   2300 mm

C4 How many litres do these containers hold?

(a)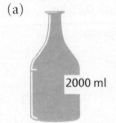

2000 ml

(b)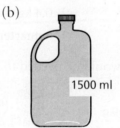

1500 ml

(c)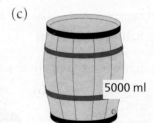

5000 ml

C5 What decimal of a litre do each of these contain?

(a) 750 ml

(b) 500 ml

(c) Milk 800 ml

(d) 100 ml

C6 How many millilitres are there in each of these?

(a) 1.5 litres   (b) 5.2 litres   (c) 10 litres   (d) 0.5 litres?

C7 How many litres are there in each of these?

(a) 3000 ml   (b) 4500 ml   (c) 650 ml   (d) 5 ml?

C8 Liquid medicine is usually given in 5 ml spoonfuls.
How many 5 ml spoonfuls are there in each of these.

(a) 100 ml   (b) 750 ml   (c) 1 litre   (d) 0.5 litres

C9 Write these quantities in order, smallest first.

750 ml   0.5 litres   1.2 litres   50 ml   1500 ml

C10 Nurses measure some medicines using a very small unit
called the **milligram** (mg).
For nurses, getting a calculation wrong could result in someone dying.

(a) Copy and complete this statement.

A milligram (mg) is .... of a gram.
There are .... milligrams in a gram.

(b) How many milligrams are there in each of these?

(i) 5 g   (ii) 50 g   (iii) 100 g   (iv) 0.5 g

(c) Write these measurements in grams.

(i) 2000 mg   (ii) 1500 mg   (iii) 500 mg   (iv) 50 mg

(d) How many milligrams are there in a kilogram?

Mega – big or what?

Sometimes *mega-* is used
in front of units.

What does *mega* mean?

This computer program needs 8 megabytes of memory.

In the UK we produce 21 megatonnes of waste a year - that's 350 kg each!

D Imperial measures

Metres, grams and litres are all part of the **Metric** system.
Until the 1970s most people in the UK used **Imperial** measurements such as
feet and inches, pints and gallons, pounds and ounces.

A ruler which measures up to 30 cm long used to be called a **foot** ruler.
About how many foot rulers can you fit alongside a metre rule?
In Imperial measurements 3 feet is a **yard**.
What can you say about a metre and a yard?

D1 Roughly how long are these distances in metres?

    (a) A long jump of 27 feet   (b) A pole vault of 18 feet
    (c) A discus throw of 210 feet   (d) A race of 100 yards

D2 Roughly how many feet are there in each of these?

    (a) 10 m   (b) 25 m   (c) 100 m   (d) 1.5 m

D3 A distance of 8 kilometres is very close to 5 miles.

    (a) 10 miles is double 5 miles, so what is 10 miles in kilometres?

    (b) Copy and complete this 'ready reckoner' table for
        changing from miles to kilometres:

Miles	5	10	20	50	100	200
Kilometres	8					

    (c) Use this table to change these distances between cities into kilometres.

        (i) York to Leeds - 25 miles   (ii) London to Dover - 75 miles

        (iii) Bristol to London - 120 miles   (iv) Glasgow to Inverness - 165 miles

        (v) Norwich to Liverpool - 215 miles

D4 To change miles into kilometres without a ready reckoner table use this rule:

Use the rule to change these distances into kilometres.

    (a) 15 miles   (b) 35 miles   (c) 55 miles   (d) 125 miles

D5 These are the distances from London to various places in the UK, in miles.

    | Salisbury 88 | Brighton 59 | Cardiff 152 | York 211 | Newcastle 285 |

    (a) Round these distances to the nearest 10 miles.

    (b) Change the rounded distances into kilometres.

D6 (a) Copy and complete this rule for changing kilometres into miles:

Miles ⟵ [ ] ⟵ | Divide by .... | ⟵ Kilometres

(b) Use this rule to change these distances into miles

(i) 24 km　　　　(ii) 48 km　　　　(iii) 88 km　　　　(iv) 136 km

D7 Change these speed limits in kilometres per hour to miles per hour

(a) **40**　　　　(b) **80**　　　　(c) **120**

If a distance in kilometres does not divide exactly by 8, then round to the nearest whole number before multiplying by 5

Example

To change 38 km into miles,　　　　$38 \div 8 = 4$ remainder 6
　　　　　　　　　　　　　　　　which is 5 to the nearest whole number
　　　　　　　　　　　　　　　　so 38 km is roughly $5 \times 5 = 25$ miles

D8 Roughly how many miles are each of these?

(a) 42 km　　　　(b) 67 km　　　　(c) 90 km　　　　(d) 130 km

D9 These continental road signs give distances in kilometres.
Copy the signs but change the distances to miles.

| Padova | 72 |
| Verona | 95 |

| Brescia | 49 |
| Milano | 52 |

| Modena | 41 |
| Ravenna | 78 |

*****D10** For many years running a mile was a popular event in athletics.

(a) Use a calculator to find what 1 mile is in kilometres.

(b) What is this in metres?

(c) In modern athletics runners can take part in a 1500 m race.
　　Is this more or less than a mile?

E Weighing up

Flour 1 kg

Tea 125 g

In the UK packets of food are sold in units of grams or kilograms by law.
In the United States however food is still sold in pounds (lbs).
A kilogram is just over 2 pounds.

E1 What are these weights roughly in kilograms?

(a) 10 lb (b) 56 lb (c) 180 lb (d) 5000 lb

(e) 3 lb (f) a half of a pound

(g) one and a half pounds

E2 Work out roughly what each of these weights is in pounds.
Do not use a calculator.

(a) 6 kg (b) 12 kg (c) 25 kg (d) 2.5 kg

(e) 7.5 kg (f) 0.5 kg (g) 600 g (h) 750 g

E3 (a) In boxing a Heavyweight is someone weighing over 190 lb.
What is this roughly in kilograms?

(b) A Flyweight is someone weighing less than 112 lb.
What is this roughly in kilograms?

E4 Mavis has a recipe for apricot jam but her scales only weigh in pounds.
Change these amounts roughly into pounds.

Preserving sugar 4 kg   Dried apricots 1.5 kg   Almonds 400 g

E5 The Olympic weightlifting record in 1996 was 1008 lb.
How much is this roughly in kilograms?

A more exact method

Hospitals weigh babies in kilograms but parents often want to know the weight in pounds.

A kilogram is very close to 2.2 pounds (lbs)

This method shows an easy way to change kilos into pounds using this.

Can you see how it works?

Use this method to find the weight in pounds of these babies:

Baby Jennifer weighs 3.5 kg	
Write down the kg weight	3.5
... and again	3.5
Write down the kgs ÷ 10	0.35
... and again	0.35
Now add these together	7.70
So the weight in pounds is 7.7 lb	

Maddi 4.1 kg   Andrew 2.7 kg   Roxanne 1.8 kg   Tulip 6.5 kg

Do you know how much you weighed at birth?

Test yourself with these questions.

T1 (a) How many millilitres of juice are there in this jug?

(b) A different jug holds 1500 ml. What is that in litres?

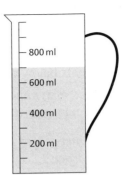

T2 Write the weights of these items in kilograms.

(a)
Pasta 1250g

(b) Frozen PEAS 2000 g

(c)
cheese 750 g

T3 The distances between these Russian towns are given in kilometres. Change these distances roughly into miles.

(a) Obayan to Belgorod 40 km
(b) Orel to Kursk 160 km
(c) Kharkov to Merefa 22 km
(d) Lubny to Piryatin 45 km

T4 Change the weights of these items into kilograms.

(a)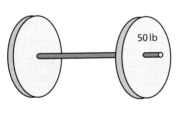
50 lb

(b)
POTATOES 112 lb

(c) Lightweight tent 7 lb

Review 2

1 Match the statements below to these shapes.

P I have 3 lines of symmetry and rotation symmetry order 3.

Q I have 1 line of symmetry and rotation symmetry order 1.

R I have 2 lines of symmetry and rotation symmetry order 2.

S I have no lines of symmetry and rotation symmetry order 1.

T I have no lines of symmetry and rotation symmetry order 2.

A   B   C   D   E

2 This shows part of a shape drawn on a coordinate grid.
   The whole shape has two lines of symmetry, the x-axis and the y-axis.

   (a) Copy the diagram.
       Add two more points and complete the shape.

   (b) Write down the coordinates of the two new points.

   (c) What is the order of rotation symmetry of the complete shape?

3 Here are three of Anna's bracelets.

   (a) Size 1 is made from 5 silver bars.
       How many bars would be needed to make a size 4 bracelets?

   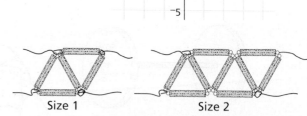

   Size 1   Size 2

   (b) Copy and complete this table.

   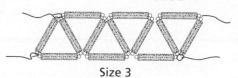

   Size 3

Size of bracelet (n)	1	2	3	4	5	10
Number of bars (b)	5	9				

   (c) Which of these expressions is correct for the number of bars (b) in a size n bracelet?

   $b = 3n + 2$ $b = 2n + 3$ $b = 5n$ $b = 4n + 1$ $b = 4n - 1$

   (d) What size bracelet will use 49 silver bars?
       Show all your working.

4 This bar chart shows the number of pictures remembered by each student in a class in a memory experiment.

Copy and complete these statements by putting a number in each space.

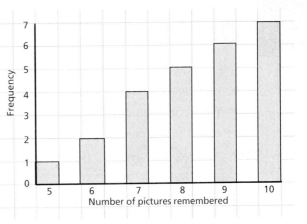

(a) ... *pupils took part in this memory experiment.*

(b) *The modal number of pictures remembered was ...*

(c) *Only ... pupils remembered less than 7 pictures.*

(d) *The median number of pictures remembered was ....*

(e) *The range of the number of pictures remembered was ....*

5 The amount of electricity used by the public goes up greatly in the evening in the intervals of a programme that a lot of people are watching on television.
This is because people all put kettles, lights and other electrical items on at the same time.
The graph below shows the electricity being used in an area of the UK one evening.

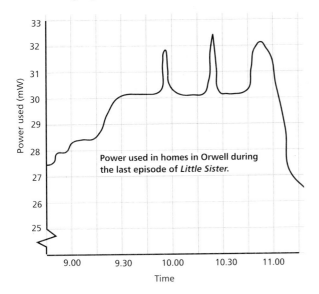

Power used in homes in Orwell during the last episode of *Little Sister.*

A megawatt(mW) is a million watts.

(a) The programme started at 9.30 and there were two intervals in the programme.
At roughly what times were these?

(b) What do you think happened between 10.45 and 11.15?

(c) For roughly how long was the amount of power being used greater than 30 mW?

6 Change these quantities into kilograms, using decimals.

(a) 2000 g   (b) 250 g   (c) 3 kg 500 g   (d) 50 g

7 What, roughly, are these Imperial measurements in metric units.

(a) 60 miles   (b) 30 yards   (c) 28 pounds   (d) $2\frac{1}{2}$ pounds

Decimals

This work will help you to

◆ read decimals from a variety of scales

◆ put decimals in order of size

◆ round to the nearest whole number and to one, two and three decimal places

◆ multiply and divide by 10, 100, 1000, ... (including converting between metric units)

A *One decimal place*

This number line is on sheet P23.

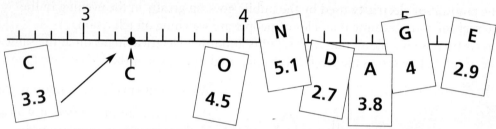

• Mark the letters on the line to spell a word.

A1 This question is on sheet P23.

A2 What number does each arrow point to?

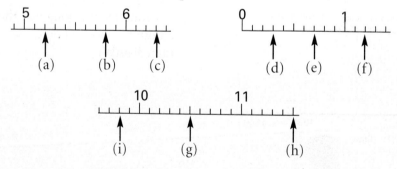

A3 This question is on sheet P23.

A4 Which of the discs will go through the slot?

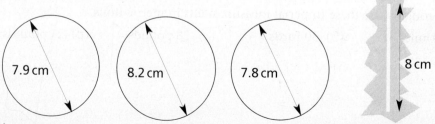

A5 Which of these numbers are between 2.2 and 4?

3.3, 2, 2.9, 4.5, 3, 3.9, 6.1, 1.9

A6 Put each list of numbers in order, smallest first.

(a) 3.4, 8.5, 7, 6.7, 1.2, 2, 0.9, 0.1   (b) 5.6, 3, 9.1, 11, 0.5, 0.2, 1.1, 4.6

A7 In a guessing contest, some students guess the length of this line.
Their guesses are:

(a) Measure the length of the line.

(b) Which guess is the closest?

A8 The numbers in this pattern go up by 0.2 each time.

0.2, 0.4, 0.6, ...

What are the next three numbers in the pattern?

A9 The numbers in this pattern go up by 0.5 each time.

0.3, 0.8, 1.3, ...

What are the next three numbers in the pattern?

A10 What number does each arrow point to?

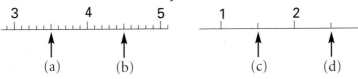

A11 Joel says this arrow points to 3.2 but James says it points to 3.4
Who is right?

A12 What number does each arrow point to?

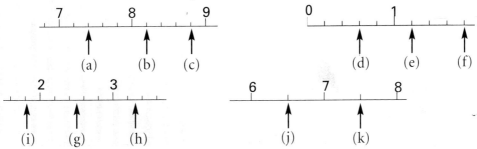

A13 This question is on sheet P23.

B And it's raining ...

A calculator may be used for this section.

B1

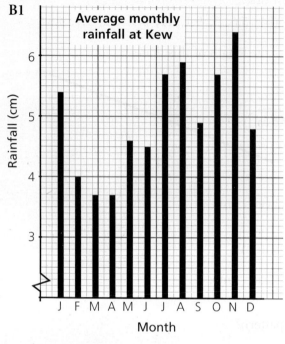

On average,

(a) What is the monthly rainfall at Kew for September?

(b) Which are the three driest months?

(c) How much rain falls in the wettest month?

(d) How much rain falls in a year?

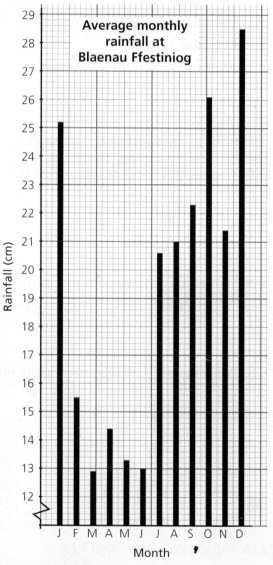

*B2 On average,

(a) What is the monthly rainfall at Blaenau Ffestiniog during

   (i) April

   (ii) February

   (iii) October

(b) What is the monthly rainfall during the wettest month?

(c) What is the difference in monthly rainfall between the wettest month and the driest month?

(d) How much more rain falls at Blaenau Ffestiniog than falls at Kew in

   (i) September

   (ii) May

   (iii) December

C Two decimal places

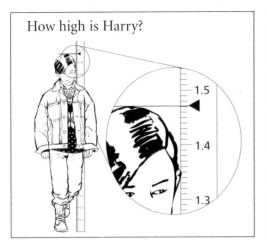

How high is Harry?

Put these cards in order, from the smallest number to the largest.

What word do you get?

A 1.52

M 1.23

F 0.09

O 0.7

U 1.4

R 1.05

L 1.50

C1 What number does each arrow point to?

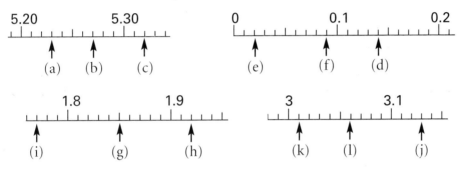

C2 This question is on sheet P24.

C3 Here are some cars.

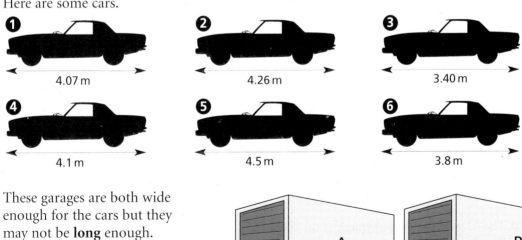

❶ 4.07 m

❷ 4.26 m

❸ 3.40 m

❹ 4.1 m

❺ 4.5 m

❻ 3.8 m

These garages are both wide enough for the cars but they may not be **long** enough.

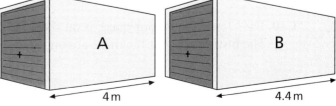

A   4 m

B   4.4 m

(a) Which cars could go in garage A.

(b) Which could go in garage B?

C4 Here are some cards…

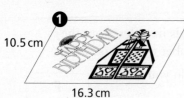

1 10.5 cm / 16.3 cm

2 9.85 cm / 16.1 cm

3 9.25 cm / 15.35 cm

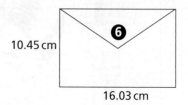

… and here are some envelopes.

A 9.3 cm / 15.5 cm

B 10.6 cm / 16.25 cm

6 10.45 cm / 16.03 cm

(a) Which cards could fit in envelope A?

(b) Which cards could fit in the other two envelopes?

C5 Which of these numbers are between 2.56 and 3.2?

2.5, 3.5, 2.67, 2.6, 2.09, 3.1, 3.19, 3.07, 3.31

C6 Put these numbers in order, smallest first.

7.1, 7.92, 8, 7.06, 7.4, 7.28

C7 Put these numbers in order, largest first.

0.45, 0.3, 1.2, 1.03, 0.46, 0.06

C8 In a guessing contest, some students guess the weight of a cat.
Their guesses are:

3.7 kg   3.85 kg   3.95 kg   3.8 kg   3.9 kg

The cat weighs 3.88 kg.

Which guess is the closest?

*__C9__ What number is half way between

(a) 3.2 and 3.4　　(b) 2.56 and 2.58　　(c) 1.2 and 1.6　　(d) 1.2 and 1.3

(e) 9.8 and 10.2　　(f) 6.23 and 6.29　　(g) 6.48 and 6.5　　(h) 4.29 and 4.33

*__C10__ The 'closest neighbour maze' is on sheet P25.
The instructions for the maze are on the sheet.

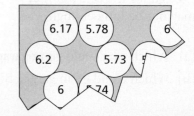

6.17   5.78   6
6.2   5.73
6   74

D Rounding to the nearest whole number

On a motorway there is a phone every kilometre.
There are distance posts every 100 metres.

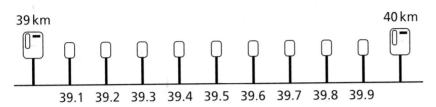

When you break down, you want to walk to the nearest phone.

- Which phone would you walk to if you broke down next to the post at 39.8?
- Which phone is nearest to 39.37 km?

D1 Which whole number is nearest to each of these?

    (a) 3.9   (b) 4.1   (c) 18.7   (d) 13.9   (e) 27.4

D2 Round these to the nearest metre.

    (a) 4.6 m   (b) 17.2 m   (c) 20.3 m   (d) 5.8 m   (e) 47.9 m

D3 Round these to the nearest kilometre.

    (a) 134.2 km   (b) 12.5 km   (c) 981.3 km   (d) 26.5 km   (e) 89.6 km

D4

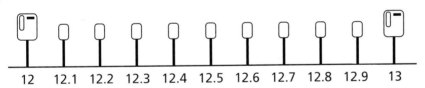

    Which phone (12 km or 13 km) is nearest to each of these?

    (a) 12.9   (b) 12.27   (c) 12.81   (d) 12.54   (e) 12.49

D5 Which whole number is nearest to each of these?

    (a) 4.83   (b) 2.34   (c) 7.88   (d) 5.36   (e) 16.75

D6 Round these to the nearest kilogram.

    (a) 5.73 kg   (b) 1.09 kg   (c) 14.64 kg   (d) 10.59 kg   (e) 18.29 kg

D7 Round these to the nearest litre.

    (a) 17.77 litres (b) 53.91 litres (c) 37.02 litres (d) 0.92 litres   (e) 15.08 litres

D8 Round these to the nearest whole number.

    (a) 6.7   (b) 31.17   (c) 53.47   (d) 19.59   (e) 0.89

E At home

This the plan of the ground floor of Gill's house.

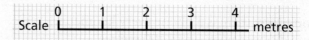

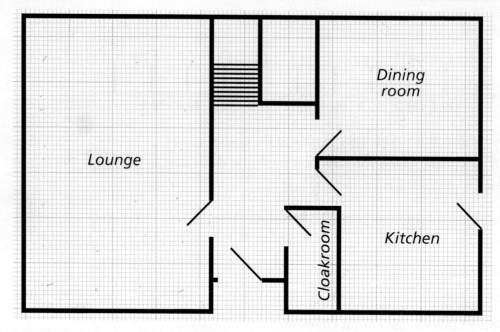

A calculator may be used for this section.

E1 (a) What is the width of the lounge?

(b) What is the length of the lounge?

(c) Work out the area of the lounge in square metres.
Write your answer to the nearest whole number.

E2 What is the area of the cloakroom, rounded to the nearest whole number?

E3 (a) What is the width of the dining room?

(b) What is the length of the dining room?

(c) Gill plans to put a picture rail at the top of each wall in the dining room.
How long will the rail be in total?

(d) She buys a large rug on holiday.
It measures 2.9 metres by 3.35 metres.
Will it fit in the dining room?

E4 A kitchen cupboard is 1.5 m long, 0.75 m wide and 1.2 m high.
Will it fit through the kitchen door?

*E5 A settee is 84 centimetres wide.
Will it fit through the door of the lounge without any twisting or turning?

F Rounding to one decimal place

Examples

Round 1.72 to one decimal place.

1.72 is between **1.7** and **1.8**

It is closer to 1.7 (the '2' tells you this) so 1.72 rounds to 1.7

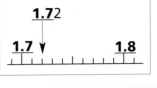

Round 3.25671 to one decimal place.

3.25671 is between **3.2** and **3.3**

It is closer to 3.3 (the '5' tells you this) so 3.25671 rounds to 3.3

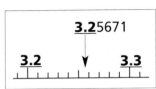

This is a simple rule for rounding to one decimal place

> If the digit in the second decimal place is
> • 5 or above, round up
> • 4 or below, round down

F1 The numbers in the rectangles are written to one decimal place in the circles. Find five matching pairs.

6.34   6.24   5.359

6.391   5.312

6.3   5.3   5.4

6.4   6.2

F2 Round these numbers to one decimal place.

(a) 1.21   (b) 5.67   (c) 0.18   (d) 12.39   (e) 14.34

(f) 4.578   (g) 9.345   (h) 12.417   (i) 0.380   (j) 1.308

F3 Round these numbers to one decimal place.

(a) 6.78324   (b) 1.5392435   (c) 7.1084623   (d) 2.0632193

F4

A	B	E	H	I	G	L	N	P	R	T	W
2.0	2.1	2.2	2.3	2.4	2.5	2.6	2.7	2.8	2.9	3.0	3.1

Round each decimal below to one decimal place and find a letter for each one. Rearrange each set of letters to spell an animal.

(a) 2.8604, 2.24, 2.138, 2.034

(b) 2.609, 2.2561, 2.1901, 1.964, 3.10131

(c) 2.51, 2.908, 2.412, 2.98, 2.1984

(d) 2.764123, 2.2461, 2.5543, 2.34452, 1.98361, 3.0499, 2.22109, 2.70671

ⓖ *Rounding to more than one decimal place*

> **Examples**
>
> Round 4.1873 to two decimal places.
>
> **4.18**73 is between **4.18** and **4.19**
>
> It is closer to 4.19 (the '7' tells you this) so 4.1873 rounds to 4.19
>
>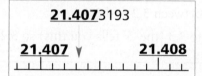
>
> Round 21.4073193 to three decimal places.
>
> **21.407**3193 is between **21.407** and **21.408**
>
> It is closer to 21.407 (the '3' tells you this) so 21.4073193 rounds to 21.407
>
> **21.407**3193
>
> **21.407** ▾   **21.408**

This is a rule for rounding decimals

> Find the column you are interested in (1st, 2nd, 3rd, ... decimal place)
>
> If the next digit on the right is   •   5 or above, round up
>   •   4 or below, round down

G1 The numbers in the rectangles are written to two decimal places in the loops.
Find five matching pairs.

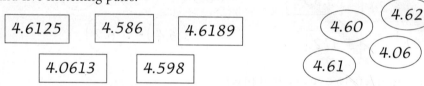

G2 Round these numbers to two decimal places.

(a) 5.631   (b) 16.126   (c) 6.401   (d) 23.089   (e) 1.325

G3 Round these to the nearest penny.

(a) £1.68123   (b) £14.92604   (c) £5.235631   (d) £26.5013964

G4 The numbers in the rectangles are written to three decimal places in the loops.
Find five matching pairs.

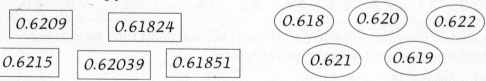

G5 Round these numbers to three decimal places.

(a) 1.4936   (b) 1.9284   (c) 3.58129   (d) 13.24561

(e) 1.59001   (f) 1.23991   (g) 15.47912   (h) 0.87978

$\boxed{H}$ *Multiplying and dividing by powers of ten*

Examples

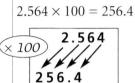

2.564 × 100 = 256.4

Multiplying by 100 moves figures two places to the left.

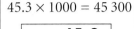

45.3 × 1000 = 45 300

Multiplying by 1000 moves figures three places to the left.

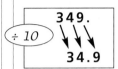

349 ÷ 10 = 34.9

Dividing by 10 moves figures one place to the right.

19.3 ÷ 1000 = 0.0193

Dividing by 1000 moves figures three places to the right.

H1 Calculate each of these.

    (a) 2.89 × 10   (b) 4.91 × 100   (c) 59.436 × 100   (d) 0.904 × 1000

    (e) 9.5 × 100   (f) 0.549 × 1000   (g) 13.2 × 100   (h) 2.31 × 1000

H2 Calculate each of these.

    (a) 46.1 ÷ 10   (b) 4290.6 ÷ 100   (c) 5932 ÷ 1000   (d) 53.2 ÷ 100

    (e) 9.3 ÷ 100   (f) 0.5 ÷ 10   (g) 13 ÷ 1000   (h) 0.12 ÷ 1000

H3 Calculate each of these.

    (a) 3.09 × 10   (b) 4.2 ÷ 10   (c) 23.41 × 100   (d) 0.21 × 1000

    (e) 54 ÷ 100   (f) 2.34 ÷ 100   (g) 1.2 × 1000   (h) 0.34 ÷ 100

H4 Find the missing number in each calculation

    (a) ■ × 10 = 67.3   (b) 678 ÷ ■ = 6.78   (c) 3.01 × ■ = 3010

$\boxed{I}$ *Metric units*

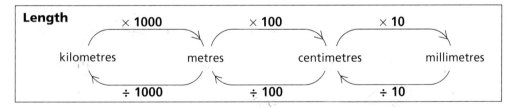

I1 **A** 1.6 × 100   **B** 1.6 × 1000    **C** 1.6 ÷ 1000   **D** 1.6 ÷ 100

    (a) Choose the correct calculation to change 1.6 km to metres.

    (b) Choose the correct calculation to change 1.6 cm to metres

I2 (a) Change 87 200 m to kilometres.   (b) Change 4.5 m to centimetres.

    (c) Change 72 mm to centimetres.   (d) Change 3.2 km to metres.

I3 Senzo's bamboo plant grows 63 cm every day.

    (a) In centimetres, how much does it grow in 10 days?

    (b) Give your answer in metres.

I4 The smallest recorded marine fish is the dwarf goby at 8.6 mm long.

    (a) In millimetres, how long is a line of 100 dwarf goby fish, placed end to end?

    (b) Give your answer in centimetres.

I5 Vincent's car is 4.5 m long.

    (a) How long is a line of 1000 of these cars, placed end to end?

    (b) York is 39 km from Leeds. Would the line of cars stretch this far?

I6 A specimen of *Dioon edule*, a Mexican evergreen shrub, was found to be growing only 0.76 mm in a year.

At this rate, how many centimetres would it grow in a thousand years?

I7 The full stops in this book are 0.5 mm wide.

How wide will a hundred of these full stops be if they are printed side by side? Give your answer in centimetres.

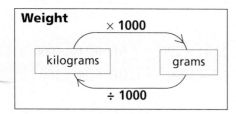

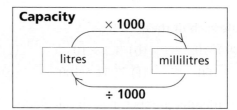

I8 (a) Change 2450 g to kilograms.   (b) Change 1.2 litres to millilitres.

    (c) Change 890 ml to litres.   (d) Change 0.3 kg to grams.

I9 Which is heavier, the cat or the hedgehog?

2.58 kg

785 g

I10 A house mouse weighs 12 g.
How much would 100 of these mice weigh in kilograms?

I11 Jane has two cartons of milk.
One carton holds 500 ml and the other holds 250 ml.

How many **litres** of milk does she have altogether?

I12 Helen buys 6 bags of flour, each holding 250 grams.
How many kilograms of flour does she buy altogether?

I13 Here are some glasses.
List them in order, starting with the one that holds the most.

 **A**  **B**  **C**  **D**  **E**

225 ml   0.175 litres   0.2 litres   150 ml   0.30 litres

I14 Sue has a bottle that holds 0.3 litres of medicine.
She takes 5 ml of this medicine every day.

How long will her medicine last?

I15 Put these weights in order, smallest first.

300 g, 0.5 kg, 0.07 kg, 67 g, 892 g, 1.04 kg, 0.985 kg

Test yourself with these questions

Do not use a calculator for questions T1 to T6.

T1 (a) The average weight for the men in a local football team is 74.85 kg.
What is this to the nearest kilogram?

(b) Round 2.36789 to one decimal place.

T2 Which arrow is
pointing to 5.02?

```
        5              5.1             5.2
├┴┴┴┼┴┴┴┴┴┴┴┴┴┴┴┼┴┴┴┴┴┴┴┴┴┴┴┼┴┴┴┴┤
        ↑              ↑               ↑
        A              B               C
```

T3 Mary has eight cats. She weighs them in kilograms.
She writes their weights in order as shown below.

One of the weights is in the wrong place.

3.3, 3.12, 3.24, 3.31, 3.52, 3.62, 3.67, 3.89

Which weight is in the wrong place?

T4 Put these numbers is order, smallest first: 2.36   2.1   2.09   2.7

T5 What is the missing number in 3.4 × ■ = 3400?

T6 A hairdresser buys a large bottle of shampoo that holds 1.5 litres.
How many millilitres of shampoo is this?

T7 Delroy bought a pack of 4 videos for £9.95.
Use a calculator to find how much each video cost him correct to
the nearest penny.

12 Evaluating expressions

You will revise

◆ how letters can stand for numbers in expressions and formulas

You will learn

◆ how to substitute in simple expressions and formulas.

A Rules for calculation

• Can you work these out?

A $(10 - 2) \times 3$

B $5 \times (3 - 1)$

C $10 + 2 \times 3$

D $5 \times 3 - 1$

E $12 - (3 + 1)$

F $\frac{6}{2} + 4$

G $\frac{6 + 4}{2}$

H $6 + \frac{4}{2}$

I $6 - \frac{4}{2}$

This means $(6 + 4) \div 2$

Brackets

• Evaluate expressions in brackets first

To calculate with +, −, × and ÷

• Multiply or divide **before** you add or subtract

• Otherwise, work from left to right

A1 Without using a calculator, work out each of these.

(a) $(6 + 3) \times 2$ (b) $3 \times (2 + 5)$ (c) $2 \times (10 - 4)$

(d) $4 \times 5 - 3$ (e) $10 + 3 \times 3$ (f) $15 - (10 - 1)$

(g) $\frac{12}{3} + 6$ (h) $8 + \frac{16}{4}$ (i) $\frac{8 + 2}{5}$

(j) $\frac{16 - 8}{4}$ (k) $\frac{20}{5} - 3$ (l) $7 - \frac{15}{5}$

A2 Evaluate each of these. (Use a calculator when you need to.)

(a) $\frac{18 - 1}{2}$ (b) $(10 + 2.5) \times 3$ (c) $\frac{12}{5} - 1$

(d) $1.5 \times (8 - 5)$ (e) $10 + \frac{3}{1.5}$ (f) $\frac{14 + 6.5}{5}$

(g) $12 - \frac{52}{10.4}$ (h) $20 + 3.2 \times 6$ (i) $5.14 + \frac{15.87}{6.9}$

A3 Find the missing number in each of these calculations.

(a) $5 \times 6 + \blacksquare = 40$ (b) $(6 + 2) \times \blacksquare = 24$ (c) $(\blacksquare - 5) \times 3 = 15$

(d) $\frac{10 - \blacksquare}{4} = 2$ (e) $\frac{\blacksquare}{3} + 9 = 14$ (f) $20 - \frac{10}{\blacksquare} = 15$

B Simple substitution

Examples

Find the value of $3(x - 1)$ when $x = 5$.

$$3(x - 1) = 3 \times (5 - 1)$$
$$= 3 \times 4$$
$$= 12$$

Find the value of $\dfrac{h - 5}{2}$ when $h = 11$.

$$\dfrac{h - 5}{2} = \dfrac{11 - 5}{2}$$
$$= \dfrac{6}{2}$$
$$= 3$$

Find the value of $\dfrac{a}{3} + 9$ when $a = 12$.

$$\dfrac{a}{3} + 9 = \dfrac{12}{3} + 9$$
$$= 4 + 9$$
$$= 13$$

B1 What is the value of each expression when $x = 4$?

(a) $x + 2$ (b) $3x$ (c) $x - 3$ (d) $\dfrac{x}{2}$

B2 Evaluate each expression when $y = 15$.

(a) $y - 10$ (b) $2y$ (c) $y + 5$ (d) $\dfrac{y}{5}$

B3 What is the value of each expression when $p = 10$?

(a) $2p - 1$ (b) $3p + 5$ (c) $2(p - 5)$ (d) $3(p + 1)$

(e) $\dfrac{p}{5} + 2$ (f) $\dfrac{p + 2}{3}$ (g) $\dfrac{p - 2}{4}$ (h) $\dfrac{p}{2} - 3$

B4 (a) Copy and complete this table showing the value of each expression for some different values of n.

	$n = 3$	$n = 6$	$n = 9$	$n = 12$
$3n + 4$			31	
$5n - 2$				
$2(n - 1)$				
$4(1 + n)$	16			
$\dfrac{n + 6}{2}$				
$\dfrac{n}{2} - 1$				

(b) (i) Which expression has a value of 40 when $n = 9$?

(ii) Which expressions have the same value when $n = 3$?

(iii) Which expressions have the same value when $n = 6$?

(iv) Which expression has the greatest value when $n = 12$?

(v) Which expression has the smallest value when $n = 9$?

*B5 Each expression in the diagram stands for the length of a side in centimetres.

   (a) (i) Work out the length of each side
        when $x = 3$ and sketch the triangle.

      (ii) What is the perimeter of your triangle?

   (b) What is the perimeter of the triangle when $x = 5$?

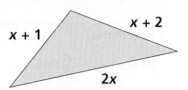

*B6 Each expression in the diagram stands for the length of a side in centimetres.

   (a) (i) Work out the length of each side
        when $x = 2$ and draw the rectangle.

      (ii) What is the area of your rectangle?

   (b) What is the area of the rectangle when $x = 10$?

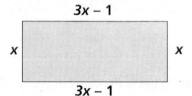

Link up four

A game for 2 players

What you need

- You need a dice.
  You need about 12 counters or tiles each.
  You need a copy of the game board shown below (sheet D132)
  You also need a set of game cards (sheet D133)

Before you start

- Deal five cards to each player
  (you do not need to keep them hidden).

When it is your turn

- Roll the dice.

- The number on the dice is
  the value of n for your turn.

- Find the value of any one of your expressions.
  Cover this number on the board
  with one of your counters.

- Discard the card you used and pick another.

- If none of your expressions gives a number on
  the board, you do not cover a number.

- You can only use **one** card on your turn.

The winner

- The winner is the first player to cover four numbers in a row
  (across, down or diagonally).

◯	3	10	◯	6
8	9	6	7	4
13	4	⬤	⬤	12
7	◯	8	⬤	9
14	6	11	1	15

C Rules

C1 Some undertakers use the rule that the length of a body is about three times the circumference of the head.

We can write this rule as

Length = 3 × circumference

(a) Use this rule to estimate the length of a body whose head has a circumference of 50 cm.

(b) Use this rule to estimate the length of a body whose head has a circumference of 54 cm.

C2 *Superstore Systems* make CD racks.
They make racks to fit any number of CDs.

The base of each rack is 60 mm high.
Each CD space adds another 14 mm to the height of the rack.

The rule for the height of the rack is

Height in mm = 14 × number of CDs + 60

Work out the height of a rack that holds

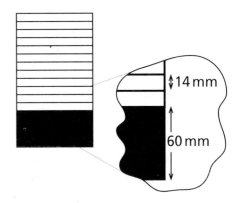

(a) 10 CDs   (b) 30 CDs

(c) 50 CDs   (d) 80 CDs

C3 There is a rule for finding how far away thunderstorms are when you know how many seconds it is between seeing the lightning and hearing the thunder.

$$\text{Distance in miles} = \frac{\text{time in seconds}}{5}$$

(a) Work out how far away away the storm is if it takes 40 seconds to hear the thunder.

(b) How far is it if you count 15 seconds between the thunder and lightning?

C4 *Superstore Systems* also make cassette tape racks.

The rule for the height of the rack is

Height in mm = 20 × number of cassettes + 40

Work out the height of a rack that holds

(a) 10 tapes   (b) 15 tapes

(c) 20 tapes   (d) 30 tapes

C5 The *Rugged Walk* outdoor centre organises walking trips.

They use this rule to work out the number of maps to take for groups of people.

$$\text{Number of maps} = \frac{\text{number of people}}{2} + 1$$

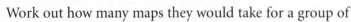

Work out how many maps they would take for a group of

(a) 10 people   (b) 16 people   (c) 30 people

C6 Pru makes dresses in a factory.
This formula is used to calculate her weekly wage.

Weekly wage (£) = 3 × *number of dresses* + 30

Work out her weekly wage for

(a) 30 dresses   (b) 60 dresses   (c) 80 dresses

C7 The number of points a soccer team has
may be worked out using this formula.

Number of points = 3 × *number of wins* + *number of draws*

Last season, Manchester United had 28 wins and 7 draws.
Work out the number of points they had.   [Edexcel]

C8 Some people work at the Pizza Parlour.
The formula used for their wages is

Weekly wage = *number of hours* × *hourly rate*

(a) Sue washes dishes for 12 hours at an hourly rate of £4.05.
How much does she earn?

(b) Fran makes pizzas at an hourly rate of £5.00 for 28 hours.
How much does she earn?

C9 Cheryl was working out the cost of hiring a van for a day.

First of all she worked out the mileage cost.
She used the formula

Mileage cost = *mileage rate* × *number of miles travelled*

The mileage rate was 8 pence per mile.
Cheryl travelled 280 miles.

(a) Work out the mileage cost.

Cheryl worked out the total cost by using the formula

Total hire cost = *basic hire cost* + *mileage cost*

The basic hire cost was £45

(b) Work out the total hire cost.   [Edexcel]

D Rules without words

Kim uses this rule to work out how many sandwiches to make for a party.

$$S = 4p + 10$$

S is the number of sandwiches and p is the number of people at the party.

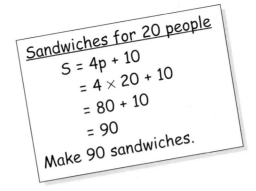

Sandwiches for 20 people
$S = 4p + 10$
$= 4 \times 20 + 10$
$= 80 + 10$
$= 90$
Make 90 sandwiches.

D1 A clothing shop uses the following rule to change British dress sizes to American ones.

$$A = B - 4$$

A is the American and B is the British dress size.

(a) Doreen wears a British dress size of 14.
What is her American dress size?

(b) Change the British size of 18 to the American size.

D2 The rule to work out the perimeter of a regular pentagon is

$$P = 5s$$

P is the perimeter of the pentagon and s is the length of one side.

Calculate the perimeter of a regular pentagon where one side measures

(a) 2 cm   (b) 7 cm   (c) 8 mm

D3 Peter uses this rule to work out how much mince to use for a cottage pie.

$$W = 100n + 80$$

W is the weight in grams and n is the number of people.

How much mince would Peter buy to make a pie for

(a) 4 people   (b) 6 people   (c) 10 people

D4 Craig's band has five members.
After each performance, the whole band is paid.

They use this rule to work out how much each band member gets paid.

$$M = \frac{F - 50}{5}$$

M is the amount of money each band member gets and F is the total the band gets for a performance.

(a) On Saturday, the band gets paid £225 for a night at Jo Jo's.
How much did each band member get?

(b) How much does each band member get if the total earned is £450?

Test yourself with these questions

T1 Evaluate each of these.

(a) $4.2 \times (3.6 - 1.35)$ (b) $\dfrac{8.6 + 6.35}{2.3}$ (c) $6.01 - \dfrac{10.64}{1.9}$

T2 What is the value of each expression when $n = 8$?

(a) $2n - 10$ (b) $5(n + 1)$ (c) $\dfrac{n}{4} + 12$ (d) $\dfrac{n + 2}{5}$

T3 Evaluate $\dfrac{12 + x}{2}$ when

(a) $x = 2$ (b) $x = 8$ (c) $x = 10$ (d) $x = 5$

T4 The *Rugged Walk* outdoor centre organises walking trips.

They use this rule to work out the number of sandwiches to take for groups of people.

$S = 3p + 5$

S is the number of sandwiches and p is the number of people.

Work out how many sandwiches they would take for a group of

(a) 5 people   (b) 10 people   (c) 16 people

13 Shopping

This work will show you how to use different charts to present data.

You will learn

◆ how to draw pie charts using percentages

◆ how to interpret and draw composite bar charts

A *In the bar*

Here is a typical label on a tub of ice cream.

Nutritional information

Energy 167 kcal per 100 g

Water	64%
Sugar	23%
Starch	2%
Protein	4%
Fat	7%

This information can be shown on a bar.

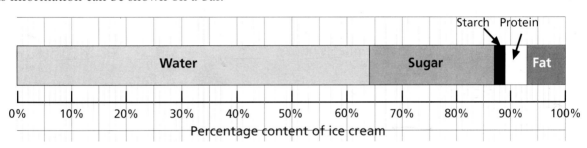

A1 This diagram shows the contents of a typical Cheddar cheese.

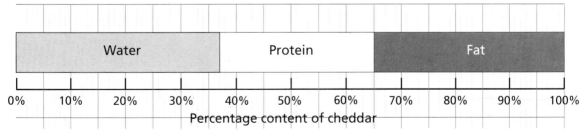

(a) What percentage of Cheddar cheese is water?

(b) What percentage of Cheddar cheese is not water?

(c) What percentage of Cheddar cheese is protein?

(d) What percentage of Cheddar cheese is fat?

A2 These percentages show the contents of cottage cheese.

Use this information to draw a chart on graph paper showing the contents of cottage cheese.

Contents

Water	80%
Protein	15%
Fat	5%

Ⓑ *In the round*

Information which uses percentages is usually shown in a round diagram called a **pie chart**.

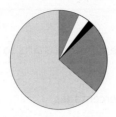

To read from or draw a pie chart you will need a pie chart scale.

Each time you want to measure a new section of a pie chart you must place the 0% on the start of a section to measure clockwise.

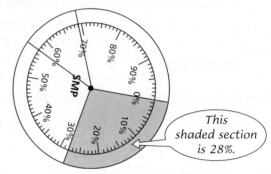

This shaded section is 28%.

Use a pie chart scale to answer these questions

B1 This pie chart shows the contents of an egg.

(a) What percentage of water does it contain?

(b) What percentage of protein does it contain?

(c) What percentage of fat does it contain?

(d) Write true or false for each of these statements:

A: An egg is almost 90% fat free

B: Around three quarters of an egg is water

C: There is more fat than protein in an egg

(e) An egg weighs about 60 g. Roughly how much of this is water?

(f) Roughly how much of a 60 g egg is fat?

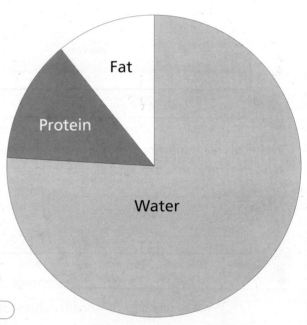

B2 Gary keeps a record of what he spends his money on over one month.
This pie chart shows what he spent money on.

(a) What did Gary spend the most money on?

(b) What percentage of his money did he spend on food and drink?

(c) What percentage of his money did he spend on going out and CDs?

(d) If Gary spent £40 that month roughly how much did he spend on going out and CDs?

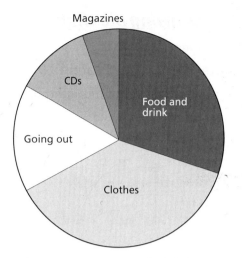

B3 This pie chart shows how the UK Government spent the taxpayers money in 1999.

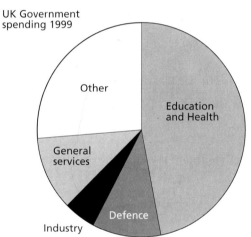

UK Government spending 1999

(a) What percentage did the Government spend on Education and Health?

(b) What percentage did the Governmemt spend on Defence?

(c) Are these statements true or false?

A: *In 1999 the Government used nearly half of all its spending on Education and Health.*

B: *In 1999 the Government used about a quarter of all its spending for Defence.*

C: *In 1999 the Government spent about twice as much on Defence as Industry.*

B4 This pie chart shows what a group of people in the UK said they spent their earnings on.

(a) What did these people say they spent their money on most of all?
What percentage is this?

(b) Did these people spend more on 'Food and drink' or on 'Housing and fuel'?

(c) What percentage did these people spend on household goods?

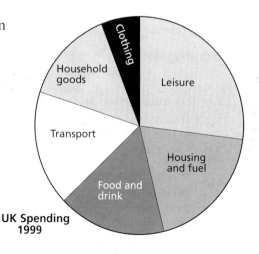

UK Spending 1999

C Drawing pie charts

The contents of a pizza are:

Water 48%   Protein 9%   Fat 16%   Carbohydrate 27%

To draw a pie chart of this information:

Draw a circle with a line from the centre	Put the scale on the centre with 0% on the line.	Mark at 48% and draw another line. Label.

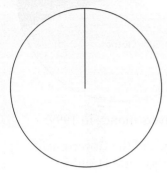  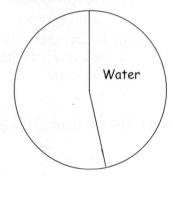

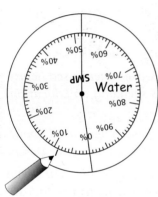

For the Protein section put the 0% on the line you have just drawn.

Mark at 9% and draw the line.

Repeat for each section.

C1 Copy and complete the pie chart showing the contents of a pizza.

Use a circle with radius 4 cm.
Label each section of your chart.

C2 This information shows how the US Government spent its budget in 1999.

Education & Health 46%   Defence 21%   Housing 3%

Industry 6%   General services 9%   Other 15%

Use this information to draw a pie chart with radius 4 cm showing how the US Government spent its budget.

C3 This information shows where the UK sold its goods abroad (its exports) in 1999.

	European Union	Other European	US/Canada	Australia New Zealand	Others
Exports	56%	5%	14%	12%	13%

Draw a pie chart with radius 4 cm to show where the UK exports its goods.

D Comparing

To compare two sets of data it is often useful to draw a **composite barchart** like this.

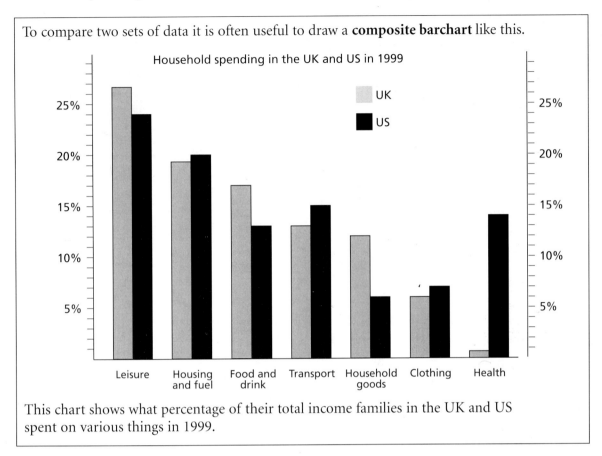

Household spending in the UK and US in 1999

This chart shows what percentage of their total income families in the UK and US spent on various things in 1999.

D1 What percentage of their income do people in the US spend on health?
Why do you think in the UK virtually no money is spent by people on health?

D2 What items did the people in the US spend a higher percentage on than in the UK?

D3 These figures show the contents of two types of cheese.

	Water	Protein	Fat	Other
Camembert	48%	23%	23%	6%
Parmesan	28%	35%	30%	7%

Use this information to draw a composite bar chart comparing the contents of the two cheeses.

Describe the differences in the contents of the two cheeses.

Test yourself with these questions

T1 Recorded music has been sold in different formats over the years. This table gives information about the UK in 1986.

Format	LP	Cassette	Single	CD
Percent	26	36	34	4

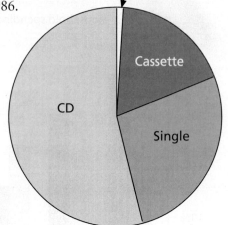

(a) Draw and label a pie chart to show this information.

This pie chart shows the sales for 1996.

(b) Make two comments about changes in the popularity of the formats between 1986 and 1996.

T2 This bar chart shows the day of the week a group of women and a group of men said they did shopping.

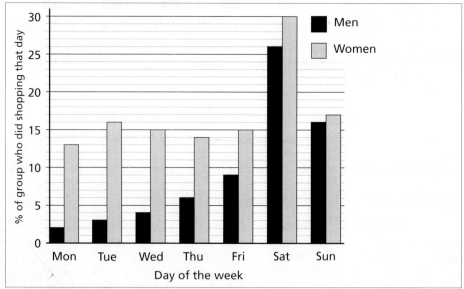

(a) Which is the most popular shopping day for the men?

(b) Give two ways in which the women's shopping is different from the men's.

14 Newspapers

You will be practising a number of skills, including

◆ rounding large numbers
◆ drawing bar charts
◆ calculating area
◆ making two-way tables

A Number search

You need a copy of a newspaper – national or local.

Try to find two examples of each of these types of number.
Write down each number you find. You could highlight it in the newspaper.

1	A number between 10 and 100	**2**	A distance in kilometres
3	An amount of money over £1000	**4**	A distance in miles
5	A person's age	**6**	A price less than £5
7	A number that has been estimated	**8**	A decimal (but not money)
9	A weight	**10**	A time given in the 24-hour clock
11	A number between 100 and 1000	**12**	A volume or capacity
13	A percentage	**14**	A fraction

B How long ago did the paper start?

The Manchester Daily Echo

No. 45276   Saturday 28 August 1998   Price 35p

This number tells you how many times the paper has appeared since it started.

Daily papers appear 6 times a week.

Get some copies of different newspapers.
From the number on the front, estimate for how many years each paper has appeared.

C **Page sizes**

National daily papers are of two main sizes: 'tabloid' (smaller) and 'broadsheet' (larger).

- Measure the length and width of a page of each type. Calculate the area of each page.

- Find the total area of all the pages of one newspaper, including any supplements.
  (Count both sides of every sheet.)

- Compare the total areas of different papers.

D **Page numbering**

Most papers are made up entirely of folded sheets.

- Pull out each sheet from a paper and look at the page numbers on it.

  Can you find any connections between the page numbers on a sheet?

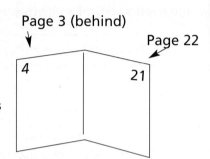

E **Costs**

- Draw a bar chart to show the prices of different daily papers.

- Draw a bar chart for the prices of Sunday papers.

- Choose a Sunday paper.
  Work out a rough estimate for the cost of buying the paper for a year.

- Choose a daily paper and estimate the cost of buying it for a year.

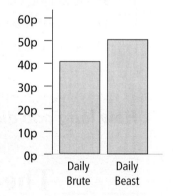

F **Graphs and charts**

- Find an example of a graph or chart in a newspaper. Cut it out, stick it in your book and write a sentence about what the chart shows.

G *Rounding numbers*

The numbers in headlines are often **rounded,** to the nearest thousand,
nearest ten thousand, and so on.

**It might be old, but this 1920 Rolls-Royce
has just 7,000 miles on its clock**
reports **David Burgess-Wise**

'**B**ODY BY
BREWSTER"
sounds like a
stage direction
from *Arsenic
and Old Lace,* and maybe
playwright Joseph Kesselring
was subconsciously influ-
enced by a coachbuilder's
plate when he chose the sur-
name "Brewster" for the
sweet little old ladies with
poisonous habits in his
corpse-strewn black comedy.

But there's nothing
remotely macabre about the
real-life body by Brewster
adorning a remarkable 1920
Rolls-Royce that's just
emerged from 66 years' con-
cealment in San Francisco,
having covered just 7,066
miles since its chassis was
shipped out of London Docks
aboard the SS Vasconia in
April 1921, bound for the old-
est and finest coachbuilder in
the United States, Brewster &
Company of New York.

**Time traveller:
the splendid
Brewster-bodied
Rolls-Royce has not
turned a wheel since
1932, when its
wealthy owner put it
into storage with
just 7,066 miles
showing on the
odometer (left).**

Unsafe airbags are blamed as Peugeot recalls 40,000 cars

THE SAFETY of all cars fitted with airbags was called into question last night after Peugeot urgently recalled 40,962 vehicles for checks on the bags. The announcement came

Fury over £11 gallon

SOME motorists faced having to pay £11.36 a gallon yesterday.

Police were called as furious drivers fought with staff at a Texaco filling station which had not advertised that it was more than doubling prices to £2.50 a litre for super.

But Paul Gizzonio, owner of the garage in Derby, denied it was a rip off. He said: "I have to make a living. And when the petrol runs out I still have to pay my staff and overheads."

G1 Make up a headline for each of these stories.
In your headline round the number as shown.

(a)
> A record crowd of 32783 were packed into City Stadium last night for the farewell concert by the Dark Angels. The group

Round to the nearest thousand.

(b)
> A record sleeve of the original pressing of Stevie Blake's 'Love Me Forever' sold for £7245 at an auction in Leeds yesterday.

Round to the nearest hundred.

(c)
> Cathy Cuddles, the film star who died last year, left all her money, which amounted to £7,654,201 to York Cats' Home.

Round to the nearest million.

(d)
> In the remote village of Little Breeding, people pay on average £734.25 a year in bus fares to and from work. This is

Round to the nearest £10.

G2 This table shows the average number of copies of Sunday newspapers sold (between March and August 2000).
This number is called the 'circulation' of the paper.

Copy the table but round each number to the nearest thousand.

Express	973 250	Observer	420 542
Independent	245 426	People	1 517 824
Mail	2 278 392	Telegraph	804 923
Mirror	1 925 571	Times	1 347 194
News of the World	4 015 147		

G3 Do as in question G2 for this table of the circulations of daily papers.

Express	1 061 873	Mirror	2 270 545
Financial Times	458 898	Star	529 574
Guardian	393 066	Sun	3 593 232
Independent	224 510	Telegraph	1 030 580
Mail	2 379 904	Times	718 672

H Mixed questions

H1 These diagrams show the sizes of some photos in a newspaper.
Calculate the area of each photo.

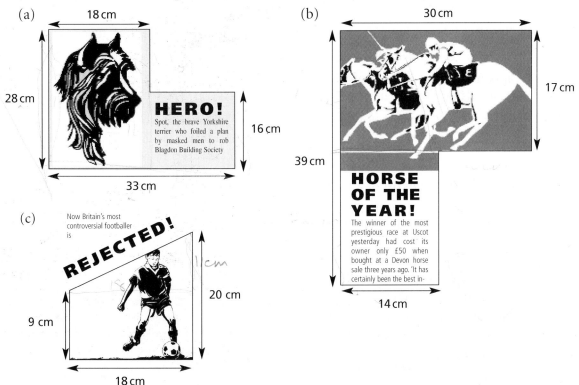

(a) 18 cm, 28 cm, 33 cm, 16 cm

HERO!
Spot, the brave Yorkshire terrier who foiled a plan by masked men to rob Blagdon Building Society

(b) 30 cm, 17 cm, 39 cm, 14 cm

HORSE OF THE YEAR!
The winner of the most prestigious race at Uscot yesterday had cost its owner only £50 when bought at a Devon horse sale three years ago. 'It has certainly been the best in–

(c) Now Britain's most controversial footballer is REJECTED!
20 cm, 9 cm, 18 cm

H2 Golda carries out a survey of the people living in her road.
She asks them whether they buy a daily paper or Sunday paper or both.

Her results are shown in this table.

	Buy daily paper	Do not buy daily paper
Buy Sunday paper	//// //// ///	//// //// //// /
Do not buy Sunday paper	//// ////	//// //// //// //// //

(a) How many people buy a Sunday paper but not a daily paper?

(b) How many people buy a daily paper but not a Sunday paper?

(c) How many people buy both a daily and a Sunday paper?

(d) How many people altogether buy a Sunday paper?

(e) How many people did Golda include altogether in her survey?

H3 Mike carried out a similar survey in his street.
As he asked each person, he wrote down D for 'buys daily paper',
S for 'buys Sunday paper', DS for 'buys both' and N for 'buys neither'.

Here are his notes.

N	S	S	DS	S	D	D	DS	N	N	N	D	S	DS	N
S	N	N	S	D	S	S	N	S	DS	DS	D	N	DS	D
N	S	S	DS	N	N	DS	D	N	DS	N	N	S	S	S

Make a table like the one above for this survey.

H4 The *Brockshire Advertiser* uses this formula to work out the price of adverts:

$$C = 15n + 80$$

n stands for the number of words in the advert.
C stands for the cost in pence.

(a) Calculate the cost of this advert.

> **Alice**, where were you on Saturday night? I waited for three hours in torment. Please be there Tuesday and keep my hopes alive.

(b) Calculate the cost of an advert with 30 words in it.

(c) Joy wants to put in an advert for her lost cat.
She has £3 to spend on the advert. How many words can she afford?

H5 This is the start of a newspaper article.

(a) Count the number of words in the first 2 centimetres of the article.

(b) The full article contains 650 words. Estimate how many centimetres it takes up.

> Film-makers are never quite sure what the cinema-going public will want next. A few years ago there was a craze for disaster movies. There will always be an audience for a love story, but a lot depends on who the stars are. Science fiction and special effects attract

2 cm

15 Drawing and using graphs

For this work you should know how to

◆ plot coordinates   ◆ work out expressions like $3 + 4n$ when $n = 2$

You will learn how to

◆ draw and interpret straight-line graphs in real-life situations

A Tables and graphs

A1 Aluna is filling a fish tank.

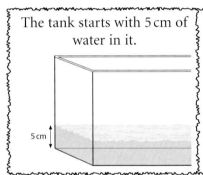

The tank starts with 5 cm of water in it.

Each minute her hose-pipe adds 2 cm.

2 cm
5 cm
7 cm

So after 1 minute, there is 7 cm of water in the tank.

(a) How deep will the water be after 2 minutes?

(b) Copy and complete this table.

Time in minutes	0	1	2	3	4	5
Depth of water in cm	5	7				

(c) On graph paper draw and label axes like these. Then plot the points from your table (the first two are shown already plotted).

(d) Join the points you have plotted. Extend the line they make.

(e) Use your graph to say how deep the water will be after 7 minutes.

(f) How deep will the water be after $3\frac{1}{2}$ minutes?

(g) How many minutes will it take until the water is 10 cm deep?

(h) Aluna starts filling the tank at exactly quarter past 3. At what time is the water 17 cm deep?

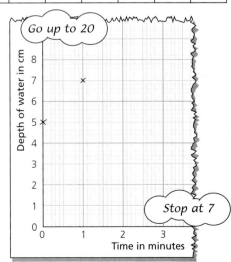

Go up to 20

Stop at 7

Depth of water in cm

Time in minutes

A2

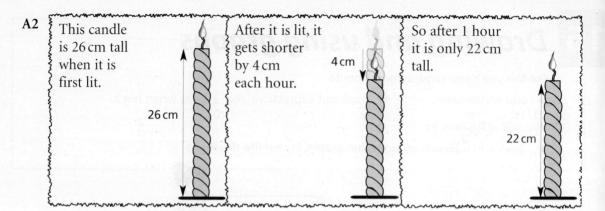

This candle is 26 cm tall when it is first lit.

26 cm

After it is lit, it gets shorter by 4 cm each hour.

4 cm

So after 1 hour it is only 22 cm tall.

22 cm

(a) How tall will the candle be after 2 hours?

(b) Copy and complete this table.

Time in hours	0	1	2	3	4
Height of candle in cm	26	22			

(c) On graph paper, draw and label axes like these.
Then plot the points from your table.

(d) Join the points you have plotted.
Extend the line they make.

(e) Use your graph to say how tall the candle will be after 6 hours.

(f) How tall will it be after $4\frac{1}{2}$ hours?

(g) How many hours will it take until the candle is 12 cm tall

(h) How long will the candle last until it goes out?

(i) If the candle was lit at half past one, at what time will it go out?

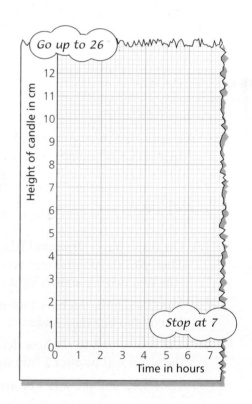

Go up to 26

Height of candle in cm

Stop at 7

Time in hours

A3 Labib is slowly heating up a liquid in a science experiment.
The liquid starts at 20°C, and heats up by 8 degrees
every 5 minutes.

(a) Copy and complete this table.

Time in minutes	0	5	10	15	20	25
Temperature in °C	20	28				

(b) Plot the points from your table on axes like
the ones below.

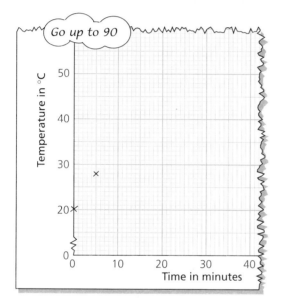

Go up to 90

(c) Join your points and extend the line.

(d) Use the graph to find out what the
temperature will be after 40 minutes.

(e) About how long will it take for the
liquid to get to 30°C?

(f) Labib needs to get the liquid to 70°C.
He starts the experiment at
a quarter past 4.
At about what time does the liquid
get to 70°C?

A4 *Chemico* make anti-freeze
for car radiators.

They test each batch of anti-freeze
by cooling a sample.

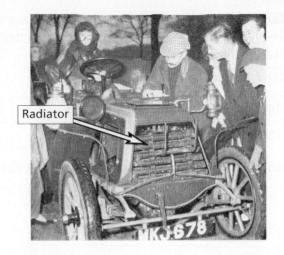

Radiator

At the start of the test, the anti-freeze is at 15°C.
Then the temperature of the anti-freeze
drops by 4 degrees each hour.

(a) What will the temperature of the anti-freeze be
after 1 hour?

(b) After 5 hours, by how many degrees will the
temperature have dropped?
What will the temperature of the anti-freeze be after 5 hours?

(c) Copy and complete this table.

Number of hours	0	1	2	3	4	5
Temperature in °C	15					

(d) Draw axes like these and plot
the points from your table.
Join the points with a line, and extend it.

(e) Use your graph to find out what the temperature
of the anti-freeze will be after $2\frac{1}{2}$ hours.

(f) What will the temperature be after 6 hours?

(g) How long will it take for the temperature
of the anti-freeze to drop to ⁻3°C?

(h) If *Chemico* start testing the anti-freeze at 10 a.m.
at what time will the temperature be ⁻7°C?

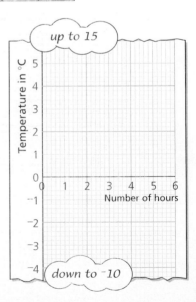

up to 15

Temperature in °C

down to ⁻10

Number of hours

B Graphs and rules

B1 You can use this rule to change miles into kilometres.

number of kilometres = number of miles × 8 ÷ 5

(a) Use the rule to check that 10 miles is the same as 16 kilometres.

(b) Work out how many kilometres there are in

    (i) 20 miles   (ii) 30 miles   (iii) 50 miles

(c) Copy and complete this table

Miles	0	10	20	30	40	50
Kilometres	0	16				

(d) Graph the points from your table using axes like these.

(e) Join the points with a line and extend it.

(f) About how many kilometres are there in

    (i) 42 miles   (ii) 55 miles

(g) About how many miles is

    (i) 20 kilometres   (ii) 75 kilometres

(h) On the road-signs below, the distances are in kilometres.
Sketch each sign with the distances written in miles.

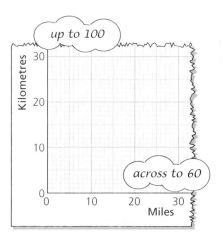

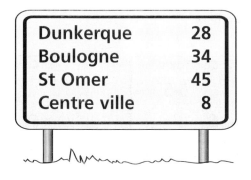

B2 *Z Car Taxis* have meters in their taxis to work out the charge for each trip.

The meters use the formula $c = 4m + 1$

c is the charge in pounds, m is the number of miles the trip takes.

For example, if a customer travels 2 miles,

$$c = 4 \times 2 + 1 = 9$$

so the charge on the meter will be £9.00

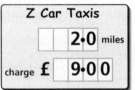

(a) Copy and complete this table showing the charge for different lengths of journey.

Miles travelled (m)	1	2	3	4	5	6
Charge in £ (c)		9				

(b) Draw a graph to show the values in your table. Draw and label your axes like this.

Plot the points from your table and join them with a line. Extend your line backwards.

Label the line *Z car taxis*.

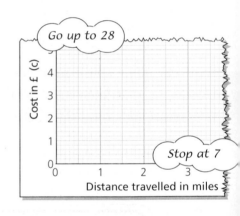

(c) Use your graph to find the missing numbers on these meters.

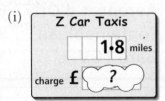

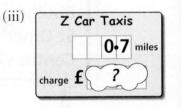

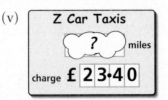

For this question, you need the graph you drew in question B2.

*B3 *Aardvark taxis* use a different formula.
Their formula is $c = 4.5 + 3m$.

So for a trip of 2 miles, $c = 4.5 + 3 \times 2 = 10.5$

The charge will be £10.50

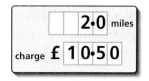

(a) Copy and complete this table for *Aardvark* taxis.

Miles travelled (m)	1	2	3	4	5	6
Charge in £ (c)		10.50				

(b) Use the values in your table to plot a graph
for the charges *Aardvark* taxis make.
Plot the graph on the same axes as for *Z car* taxis.
Label the line *Aardvark taxis.*

Use your graphs to answer these questions.

(c) (i) How much do *Z cars* charge for a trip of 1.5 miles?

(ii) How much do *Aardvark* charge for the same distance?

(d) Which is cheaper, *Z cars* or *Aardvark* , for a trip of 1.5 miles?

(e) Which is cheaper, *Z cars* or *Aardvark* , for a trip of 4.5 miles?

(f) For one distance, *Z cars* and *Aardvark* charge the same.
What distance is that?

(g) Copy and complete this advice:

Z car taxis   01979 345 123
Aardvark taxis 01979 387 395
Phone ▓▓▓▓ for journeys over ▓▓▓ miles as they are cheaper.

T1 *Computer Helpline* give help to computer users over the phone.
They use a formula to work out the charge.
The charge is based on how many minutes long the phone call is.

  Charge in pounds = number of minutes × 3 + 5

So if a call is 2 minutes long, the charge is £2 × 3 + 5 = £11.

(a) Copy and complete this table.

Number of minutes	1	2	3	4	5	6
Charge in £		11				

(c) Draw a graph to show the values in your table.
   Draw and label your axes like this.

   Plot the points from your table and
   join them with a line.

   Extend your line backwards.

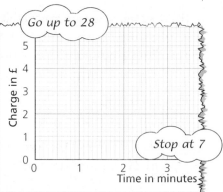

(d) Use the graph to say how much *Computer
   Helpline* charge for a $3\frac{1}{2}$ minute call.

(e) Alix makes a call. The charge is £21.50
   How long was her call?

(f) Use your graph to find the missing numbers on these bills.

(i)
Computer Helpline

Length of call
  (?) minutes

Our charge £6.50

*Helpline
for
Happy Help*

(ii)
Computer Helpline

Length of call
  (?) minutes

Our charge £18.50

*Helpline
for
Happy Help*

(iii)
Computer Helpline

Length of call
  $6\frac{1}{2}$ minutes

Our charge £ (?)

*Helpline
for
Happy Help*

Review 3

1 What number does each of these arrows point to?

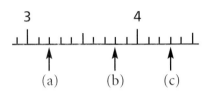 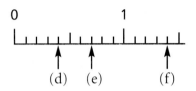

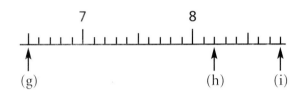 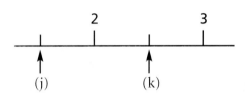

2 Put each set in order, smallest first.

(a) 1.25, 1.4, 1.03, 1.15, 1.1   (b) 0.05, 1, 0.7, 0.09, 0.11, 0.20

(c) 500 g, 0.7 kg, $\frac{1}{4}$ kg, 99 g   (d) 35 km, 5 m, 450 cm, 0.01 km, $\frac{1}{2}$ km

3 (a) What number does each arrow point to on this scale?

(b) Sketch a copy of the scale on the right. On your sketch draw and label arrows pointing to 3.55, 3.60 and 3.49 .

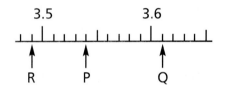

4 (a) Jo uses 450 grams from a 1 kg bag of flour. How much is left?

(b) Harry walks for $1\frac{1}{2}$ km and runs a further 300 m. How far has he gone altogether?

(c) My watering can holds 8.5 litres. I water 8 plants with 100 ml of water each. How much water is left in the can?

5 What is the value of each of the following expressions when p = 8?

(a) $3p - 1$ (b) $3(p - 1)$ (c) $p - \frac{1}{2}$ (d) $\frac{p-2}{3}$ (e) $\frac{p}{2} - 3$

6 *The Walking Company* organises rambles.
They use a rule to work out how long each ramble will take.

The rule is $T = \dfrac{d}{3} + 1$. (*T* is the time in hours; *d* is the distance in miles.)

(a) How many hours will a 6 mile ramble take?

(b) The *Lakeland* ramble is 15 miles. How long will it take?

(c) The *Marathon* ramble is 24 miles. How long will this take?

You need a pie chart scale for questions 7 and 8.

7 This pie chart shows how women with jobs
spend their time during the week.

(a) What percentage of their week
do these women spend at work?

(b) What percentage free time do they have?

(c) What percentage do they spend doing
housework, shopping etc?

(d) There are 168 hours in a week.
About how many hours are spent doing
housework, shopping etc?

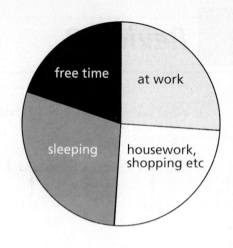

8 Men with jobs spend 29% of the week at work,
15% doing housework, shopping etc, and 29% sleeping.
The rest of the week is free time.

Draw a pie chart to show this information.

You need graph paper for question 9.

9 *Happy B* day supply birthday presents by post.
They work out the delivery cost using the formula

delivery cost in £ = weight of package in kg ÷ 2 + 3

(a) What is the delivery cost of a package weighing 10 kg?

(b) Check that the delivery cost of a 5 kg package is £5.50

(c) Copy and complete this table.

Weight	5	10	15	20	25	30
Delivery cost	5.50					

(d) Graph the points from your table,
using axes like these.

(e) Join your points with a line.
Extend your line.

Use your graph to answer these questions.

(f) About how much is the delivery cost
for a package weighing 8.5 kg?

(g) About how much is delivery for a 35 kg parcel?

(h) Alke had to pay £11.50 delivery for a package.
About how much did the package weigh?

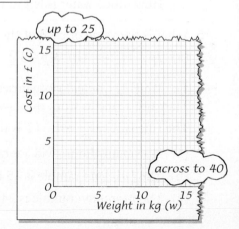